ONCE AROUND THE SUN

With my best wishes,

Rick Main

RICK MARSI

ONCE AROUND
THE SUN

Illustrated by Jan Marsi

PURPLE MOUNTAIN PRESS
Fleischmanns, New York

First Edition, 1992
published by
Purple Mountain Press, Ltd.
Main Street, P.O. Box E3
Fleischmanns, New York 12430-0378

Grateful acknowledgment is made to the Binghamton Press & Sun-Bulletin, and to Bernard M. Griffin, Publisher. This selection of columns first appeared there in the same or slightly altered form between 1987 and 1991. Many of the illustrations accompanied the first publication as well.

Library of Congress Cataloging-in-Publication Data

Marsi, Rick.
    Once around the sun / Rick Marsi ; illustrated by Jan Marsi. --
1st ed.
        p.   cm.
    Selection of columns that first appeared in the Binghamton
press & sun-bulletin between 1987 and 1991.
    ISBN 0-935796-36-3 (paperback)
    1. Natural history. 2. Natural history--Outdoor books.   3.
Nature study.   I. Marsi, Jan.   II. Title.
QH81.M2675   1992
508--dc20   92-37300
                                                            CIP

Manufactured in the United States of America

CONTENTS

PART ONE: AROUND THE SUN

PART TWO: OTHER PLACES

PART THREE: OTHER FRIENDS

PART ONE
AROUND THE SUN

January

NOISE JUNKIES ENSLAVED

These are trying times for active souls, these days of cold and darkness. Dawn breaks slowly, muddy gray. A sodden mass of oatmeal clouds drips moodily over the trees. Stay in bed—that's the message. If you get up, just make for the couch, put your feet up and let 50 channels think for you.

Who, after all, would go out on a day so devoid of inspiration? What could be out there, besides clammy cold and the blues because winter's so long?

As it turns out, there's quiet, which — if humans had more of it — would contribute mightily toward world peace. It's ironic, however. The louder life gets, the more loath we become to step out where the noise can't get to us. Silence intimidates people now. "Noise Junkies Enslaved" — that's our title these days, our senses assaulted by sound and light shows from the boob tube police and their goons.

Turn if off; break the mold; get your coat; make a run for the cold. Get in touch with your thoughts. Yes, you can think; you'd merely forgotten. When you come back, the people you left will make note that you're calm.

Aside from the quiet, a glum day outdoors holds a hatful of other delights. If you walk in the woods, you'll hear intermittent sounds that can soothe frazzled souls: trees creaking softly, wind sifting through hemlocks, squirrel claws on a carpet of leaves.

You'll hear crows calling crows to come see the big hawk they all hope will vacate the woodlot. A stream will gurgle, a brook will babble, their aqueous currents creating nature's answer to elevator music. There's a difference between this and real elevator music. If you're wearing wool pants and three layers of sweaters, you can lie by the stream in the snow and be carried away. Elevator music in real elevators doesn't carry one anywhere. Gurgling stream songs transport you to soft, relaxed places.

Enveloped in quiet, every sound in the woods makes a statement on dark winter days. There's a chickadee calling. I hear the soft whistle of kinglets high up in the pines. A turkey's wingbeats thunder out of a hemlock. A B-52, it flaps off through the gloom toward another, less frequented, roost.

Snowflakes start falling, the granular kind. They make sounds you can hear when they bounce off leaf litter that's frozen rock-hard by the cold.

Look through the branches. It seems you can see twice as far on a raw leafless day. Squirrel nests, bird nests, tree trunks that woodpeckers have ravaged — all encourage inspection, their camouflage gone with the falling of October's leaves.

Somewhere outside, within 100 feet of your dwelling, there's a bird's nest that's ripe for perusal. If deer mice haven't claimed it for winter by doming the top with plant fibers, you can pull it from shrubby recesses and ponder its deep mysteries.

What bird did you see every day in the summer? What bird built so close to the house without letting you know? How did it snap off the twigs of thorn apple to make the nest's course outer layer? From whence came the delicate rootlets that line the nest's cup? And where did the bird find that lone piece of plastic? Why would clear plastic make sense in a nest?

A catbird was near you all summer and did this. It is now in the tropics and you're not, but you do not care. You have found inspiration in overcast days and will make them work for you this winter.

ROAD CRUISING: A PRIMER

As temperatures plummet and car heaters fail, we must take outdoor thrills where we find them. That sometimes means road cruising, a form of motorized snoopery that draws its adherents toward farm fields that look like the tundra.

Would you like to road cruise? Don't say "yes" without thinking. This isn't some walk through the park. Cruising takes patience, reflexes, resolve. It means driving roads God doesn't want people on until spring.

Both sexes can do it, which I find attractive. Men who have gone out and conquered bad roads come back feeling like they are real men. Ladies who do it combine traits the men find alluring. Not only are they sensitive to beauty, but they're tough as the winter is long.

Surprisingly, when I touted road cruising on the lecture circuit recently, I met with a muted response. People are skeptical. They view driving in winter as something that cannot be fun. They're right — when it's on a four-lane with big trucks bearing down bent for glory. But when a dirt road offers looks at wild turkeys, creeping down one can chase blues away.

How does one practice this time-honored art properly? Like living a happy life or doing well at the office, successful road cruising depends on a clearly focused mission that reflects achievable goals and concentrates on their realization.

Let's focus on roads for a moment. A cruiser's life mission where roads are concerned is to find one nobody is on. "Think small" is the key concept here. If you start on a four-lane, get off. If you're on a two-lane made of blacktop with yellow lines, look for blacktop without yellow lines. When you feel dirt beneath you, you're almost home free.

Only one thing is better: a "seasonal" dirt road with signs at both ends saying "No maintenance — Nov. 1 through March 31." That means they don't plow it, so you venture beyond at your peril. It also means few, if any, houses will blight this dirt road with that blend of trashed cars and mean dogs one can meet in the country.

Obviously, a four-wheel-drive vehicle helps in such remote environs. Too many drivers of low-slung sedans have gone cruising and never come back. One reason is ditches that fill up with snow. Once they are full, they just lie there — like roadside tiger traps — waiting for cars to fall in.

Any high-riding four-wheel-drive vehicle will provide the clearance and traction you'll need to avoid getting mired, but a pickup truck surely is best. If you drive a pickup, all the other truck drivers — who are farmers and well drillers and artificial inseminators — will wave when they pass you. They won't think that you're up to no good.

But enough of preliminaries. I still haven't told you what's great about rutted dirt roads. It's seeing birds on them, and how good you feel when you do.

The season is early, yet I've already scored. Seeking corn fields on hilltops (with no traffic to scare things away), I've seen snow buntings, rough-legged hawks and horned larks. All three species sweep down from their tundra locales and find open farm country appealing.

Rough-legs in their light and dark phases are stunning — much bigger than red-tailed hawks; more likely to let you get close. They perch by the roadside, impervious, while winds whip through corn rows and drifts pile along the roadside. When a mouse ventures forth, the hawks lift off and hover, then drop with their gold talons poised.

Watching this sure beats what TV can offer. When flocks of snow buntings lift up off a field, like pure snowflakes, I think the same thing.

Creeping along at 5 mph, sipping something that's hot from a thermos, you can watch turkey flocks walking through open fields, their fear dulled by the hunger they feel. On another road you can watch starling hoards swarm on a freshly dumped heap of corn silage. Dozens pick through it, like mice crawling over piled grain.

That's it; that's road cruising. Decide on your own if you'll go. Be careful out there if you take the big step. I'm the first to admit I'm addicted.

THE PATH SELDOM TRAVELED

For someone to do something stupid, there ought to be justified cause. Are short-eared owls cause enough? For a look at these birds, would you take a dirt road that might strand you 10 miles from nowhere? Here's hoping the thought might make sense.

So what if the sign says they don't plow this road from November until winter's over. Who cares if it's rutted, and glass-smooth ice floes funnel down it like glaciers descending?

It's getting dark, isn't it? Your time is not long. Short-eared owls are daytime hunters, buff-colored shapes slicing low over fields, seeking voles that have ventured from tunnels.

The hour before dark is a prime time to see them. As a shortcut, this road represents your only hope of reaching the lonely farm field, near the lonely farmhouse, where the owls have been spotted this winter.

Go for it. How bad can this little road be? True, it starts out climbing upward and has the word "hill" in its name. Granted, seasonal roads such as this hardly ever boast year-round abodes where people whose trucks are in ditches can go for assistance. But life is adventure; life is to spin that big wheel.

I seized life that day. I was dumb, but I seized it.

The four-wheel-drive truck climbed the hill in low gear, its transmission growling as if I were pulling big logs. Go, baby; climb, baby — don't fail me now. Up, ever upward, it labored — through ruts, over ice, smashing ridges of hoarfrost with loud crunching sounds.

To the right, winter fields slumbered cowless and quiet, their weeds poking up through the snow. On the left, red pine stands dangled cones down for takers, hoping grosbeaks would find them and stay.

There were no human beings, only chains across roads where a cottage might beckon come June. When I stopped and got out at the top of the hill, I heard nothing through thick flakes that fell.

What a beautiful place come the springtime, I thought. Meadowlarks will be here, filling high fields with whistles. Bluebirds will dot fenceposts, on watch for the odd spider warming its legs in the sun. Hawks will be circling; does will give birth amid ferns at the cool forest's edge.

A tide will be surging. The rush to live life will transform this hilltop from a silent tableau to chaos.

I liked the tableau as it was, however. I liked the stark landscape I saw. If only we all had some space we could run to when problems threaten to rise up to engulf us. Silent fields in the snow put the grind in perspective. A rutted dirt road — all alone — is a tonic of sorts.

What goes up must come down, and the trip down that hill was quite scary. Not terrifying, but the specter of trucks off in ditches reared up and tied knots in my gut all the while. The road narrowed slightly; descent seemed much steeper. The ruts seemed much deeper somehow.

As it opened into a corn field and the lights of scattered farmhouses twinkled in the darkening valley below, the cowpath I was negotiating turned from packed snow to ice. The last quarter mile sparked continual prayer as the Ford inched past tawny corn stalks.

The owls were not home, by the way, when I got there. I waited through dusk, strained my eyes, said more prayers—all for naught.

"Take a right at the church, then follow that dirt road until it ends," my source had told me, describing where owls had been seen. Her directions were perfect, but the road didn't end, actually. When I got to the owl spot, it kept going, but a sign saying "Seasonal Road" explained why it lay trackless beyond that point, icy and covered with snow.

Things looked so serene up that seasonal road where I waited for owls in the gloaming. I will drive it some day when the ice melts a bit, and it's warm.

ON COLD AND WILD ANIMALS COPING

If sunlight could shine on just one drop of water, I'd like it shine on a goldeneye duck—on a fat drake the moment it pops up from diving and water rolls down off its face.

Sliding past feathers as glossy as emeralds, the droplets take on all that green and reflect it. They glide past the drake's round white cheek patch and plop in the river.

Lord, what a beautiful duck in the winter—green on the face, green and white on the body, its compact form diving in black river water, then bobbing back up like a cork. In between dives, the drake extracts oil with its bill from a gland at the base of the tail.

Then it preens every feather, so water beads up and fat ducks can pretend there's no winter.

Cold doesn't phase them—not with those feathers. As long as the river stays open, they'll be here, diving for minnows and strands of submerged vegetation.

If sub-zero nights pile upon one another, and sullen ice chunks clog the channel from somewhere upstream, the ducks will abandon me. They may fly only 10 or 20 miles downstream to a place where the current still flows unimpeded. They'll come back when winds blow from the south, a bit warmer, and they feel the north woods in their bones.

For these birds are northerly ducks, tough survivors. You'll find them in summer on lakes in the Maine wilderness. You'll see them on remote Adirondack Mountain ponds, where they pair up to build nests in tree cavities, laying olive-green eggs on a thick bed of down and wood chips.

Come winter they fly south as far as they must, but no farther— the North is their place. Some stay on the Great Lakes all winter; others on the St. Lawrence River. As long as there's water and food, they will shun southern climes.

Imagine—they stay in the North when their wings could transport them to lands where the palms swing and sway. They've adapted, adjusted. It's no big deal, really. Their bodies are tuned to the season.

Every walk that I take in the woods and the fields shows me other souls coping with winter:

Great horned owls sometimes crouch on the frozen carcass of an animal they've killed a day or two before. The heat from their bodies helps thaw out the rock-solid meat.

Ruffed grouse grow horny comblike growths on their feet that turn toes into snowshoes, enabling the birds to walk on top of the snow, where they nip aspen buds to survive. When night falls, grouse dive into two-foot snow drifts, where their body heat can raise the temperature of their insulated snow chambers some 60 degrees above that of the outside air.

Chickadees sleep deep within evergreens, in a race with the dawn to survive. To maintain their 108-degree body temperature over-night, they must consume 20 times more food on a cold day than on a warm one. When night falls, they sleep and their stored fuel is burned. Birds that go to their roosts with a build-up of fat on their sternums wake up with that fat layer gone.

It's a tough world out there with the temperature dropping. We're so ill-prepared with our toes getting cold and our bare skin exposed to the wind. Give me a goldeneye duck in the winter. Give me a creature inured to the winter; a survivor decked out for the cold.

February

PHIL'S A FRAUD

Punxsutawny Phil is a fraud. I would have exposed him BEFORE Groundhog Day, but I thought you all knew he was bogus.

I was wrong. The day after Groundhog Day, a friend let it slip that he really thought woodchucks woke up in the dead of winter, climbed out of their burrows and started to think springlike thoughts.

All these years this person had been deluded by a chamber of commerce in Punxsutawny, Pennsylvania, and the microwaved woodchuck its members exhume from a heated burrow each February 2.

Real woodchucks don't relish bear hugs from car dealers in top hats. Real woodchucks sleep like the dead until March rolls around.

Here's a woodchuck primer I hope will prevent future misconceptions. Throughout the text, I'll use woodchuck and groundhog interchangeably, because both are the same rodent creature.

As for disclaimers, there's one: Never say never, with groundhogs or anything else. Once in a blue moon, a woodchuck will use up its stored fat reserves and wake up in early February. If that happens, there had better be a human being waiting in the wings with fresh lettuce, or one skinny woodchuck will die.

But let's address rules, not exceptions. The rule says woodchucks know nothing of winter. Especially in the northern states, they hibernate from November through February.

If you followed the Appalachian Mountains south to Georgia — the southern limit of the woodchuck's range — groundhogs there would probably wake up a bit earlier and stay awake a bit later in fall.

They still would hibernate, however. If you dug them from their burrows February 2 and bounced them like basketballs, they would snooze through it all, never waking.

Let's follow a woodchuck from September through March. We'll watch as it fattens, then thins out, then fattens again.

In September most woodchucks start fattening up for the winter. Autumn's shortening days send them on a plant-eating binge that can bulk up especially healthy specimens to 10 pounds or more.

By the time hibernation ends in early March, these same woodchucks will weigh half that amount, their fat reserves used up to keep them alive during hibernation.

As for when they dig into their burrows for sleeping, mid- to late October is the usual time. One groundhog to a burrow, they block up the entrance, curl up and fade out for the season.

Their metabolic rate plummets. Their breathing slows. Body temperature drops from around 100 degrees to 38 degrees. Think about your own temperature under similar conditions. If it dropped that far, someone could drop-kick you the length of a football field, and you wouldn't come out of it, either.

Around the end of February, woodchuck body clocks start ringing in snooze alarm mode. Maintenance systems start rising toward functional levels. Blood begins flowing, not creeping like petrified sludge.

Male woodchucks respond by clambering from their burrows and seeking out burrows where females might welcome advances. Young woodchucks are born a month later and stay in the den for another five weeks after that.

So there lies the truth: Woodchucks don't surface until winter's back has been broken. In Punxsutawny, Pennsylvania, and other northeastern locations, that means early March, a full month after Microwave Phil has emerged and the chamber of commerce has cheered.

IN DEFENSE OF AN AVIAN VIRUS

Talk about a long winter — I showed an interest in starlings the other day. That doesn't usually happen. Usually, I try to dislike them and pretend they're not there.

But how many times can one prowl for great birds, come on nothing but starlings and ignore them? After the fifth such outing, during which lovable native species such as waxwings and horned larks escaped me, I weakened and watched starlings live.

There they were, 30 starlings perched up in a tree. They always hang out in flocks, these bully birds do. They're always looking for some hapless bluebird to boot out of a hole in a tree.

I still harbored ill feelings; I couldn't help it. One doesn't spend 20 years lamenting the demise of bluebirds and then soften on starlings in seconds. And bluebirds aren't the only ones.

In their lust to build nests in the limited number of cavities nature provides, starlings have evicted tree swallows, great crested flycatchers, purple martins and even woodpeckers, which is especially shameful because woodpeckers dig their own holes.

Spreading like an avian virus through the nation, starlings haven't looked back since their introduction into Central Park in 1890. Now every state has them. Their numbers have grown every year since they arrived. No natural check has been found that can stop them.

There they were in a tree in a farmer's front yard. I parked and watched. I got my camera out. It really had been a long winter.

Funny thing, though. They got interesting. First of all, they took off at the very same time, wheeled in perfect unison over a half-frozen pasture, then landed not far down the road. Walking in short, jerky steps—staying quite close together—they combed the brown earth for weed seeds. All the while they chirped, chattered, squeaked and wolf-whistled.

Several times while I watched, something spooked them and made them take flight. Up they went all together, first forming a tight ball, then suddenly drifting apart. Upon landing again, they resumed their food march, always heading in just one direction.

Periodically, the birds in the rear would fly up, flutter over their flock mates and set down again up in front. This changing of positions took place with such flowing regularity as to create the effect of a flock rolling over the field.

I took several pictures; I stared through the lens. The birds didn't look all alike. Some of their bills had turned yellow; others showed grayish brown. Some birds featured specks on their feathers, while others looked more glossy black.

OK, they were interesting. I went back to the house and read up on the way they do things.

Starlings fly in tight clumps and then revert to a looser formation to confuse hawks that might be attacking. All their rattles and squeaks indicate they're good mimics; they can imitate bobwhites, killdeer and phoebes.

Their bill colors change toward the end of winter. By the first days of spring, every beak will have turned a bright yellow. Also, by spring, those white flecks on the tips of their feathers will have worn off, revealing a purplish-black breeding plumage.

Half of their food is insects, I learned. They eat Japanese beetles and cutworms and other crop pests.

Wait a minute. Wait just a darned minute. Can I be warming toward starlings? Please come quickly, spring. I need bluebirds and swallows to get my priorities straight.

DON'T TALK ROMANCE

Black widow spiders don't celebrate Valentine's Day. Without fanfare, the females chew up their male mates and move on with the business of life.

Porcupines, too, eschew matters romantic. Females flatten their quills, let creation transpire, then suggest males depart with a thousand sharp-pointed reminders.

Romantic? No way.

Love is strictly for humans, an amorous maze based on agonizing thought processes such as, "Does she adore me? Perhaps I should buy her some flowers."

Only people get lost in that house of emotional mirrors. Beasts in the wild court, but leave out the notion of love.

That's not to say non-humans find courtship boring. Birds, for example, display for their mates in a dizzying number of ways. Given a chance, most humans would love to choreograph these routines into their own courtship rituals.

Some people actually succeed, albeit unwittingly, in mimicking animal displays. Last May, for example, I found myself on an island off the Central American coast, in a tavern where courtship ran rife.

Males of the species were displaying for females. Vocalizations filled the air, as males brayed, preened and gurgled.

"Strikingly similar to courtship behavior in the wandering albatross," I thought, taking copious notes.

While I watched, several men clanked their glasses with ladies. Wandering albatross pairs like to rattle their bills during courtship. Then couples began dancing, which got me to thinking of grebes on a vast prairie slough.

Western grebes dance on water, together, in courtship. It helps firm the pair bond.

Skittering across the surface, side by side, these two-foot-tall birds arch their necks, hold their wings out stiffly and motor along with their feet. Gaining speed, their sleek bodies stand nearly erect, and their bills point straight toward the sky.

This bar in Belize featured break dancers doing just that. Their feet skittered along, going nowhere so fast they seemed blurred in the tavern's soft light.

One dancer leapt up, did a twist in mid-air, then collapsed on his haunches again. "By George, whooping cranes!" I exclaimed when I saw the display.

That's what cranes do: They jump for each other. First they face off and bow graciously. Then they leap in the air, their legs bouncing like pogo sticks, wings flapping like flags in a breeze.

It was all there that night, as Belizean zephyrs blew in off the reef and refreshed us. I even saw ritualistic feeding, a phenomenon I hadn't witnessed since a Lake Ontario tern expedition in the early 1980s.

Terns are related to gulls, except their flight is more graceful, their bodies are sleeker and their tails feature very deep forks. Their courtship rituals normally occur on rocky nesting islands, where tern males feed females and things progress well after that.

It's a simple enough process: The female sits on a rock, flutters her wings and opens her mouth to be fed. The male pops in a fish, and — voila! — a pair bond has been formed.

As the ornithology texts explain it, the terns need to exchange these symbolic gifts in order to stimulate sexual urges. Cardinals, bluejays and cedar waxwings also engage in similar feeding rituals. There's a family of flies that does it, too, but no mammals partake — except humans.

They were serving small chunks of smoked grouper that night in the bar, while romance ebbed and flowed. Males speared chunks with toothpicks, young ladies accepted and nature transcended the difference between birds and men.

IF THE WORLD'S EVERY JUNCO SURVIVED

A killer swept by, and the world turned to silence. A Cooper's hawk knifed through suburban backyards, and the songbirds fell mute and immobile.

Strange that a fear such as this could grow there. This was a civilized complex of houses, where humans tried hard to get on with their neighbors and violence seemed out of place. Children played basketball, autos got washed, people stocked their bird feeders. Gentleness ruled where a killer would land for the day.

Tinkling songs must have drawn its attention. Perhaps flitting shapes caught its eye as it flew overhead. Neighborhoods these days boast feeders galore and lure songbirds like proteinaceous magnets. Predators, too, find themselves homing in, needing meat to stave off death and cold.

As big as a crow—short of wings, long of tail—the Cooper's hawk cut through back yards, keeping low to the ground. At the edge of one yard, a blue spruce promised darkness. A hawk could look out from its darkened recesses and never be seen by songbirds feeding 10 feet away.

Without slowing down, the hawk locked up its wings and set straight for the tree and seclusion. As it passed through the yard, feeding songbirds sprayed up from the ground where cracked corn served as bounty.

The killer ignored them, knifed straight for the tree and was swallowed by evergreen needles.

That's when I left, being stuck in my truck on the street with no premise to loiter. "Who's that guy in the street, staring into our yard? He's got field glasses. Call the police." Such a scenario just might transpire if I stayed to watch predation happen.

So I left and imagined what might occur next. There were numerous options to ponder.

First, would the hawk capture prey in the yard? Would it wait until juncos began coming back, until all seemed tranquil and bird brains had forgotten its presence? Would it dash from the spruce, short wings driving it forward, talons outstretched to pierce and to kill?

And what if it chased down a songbird and killed it? Would the hawk then dismember its prey in full view of the house? Cooper's hawks often do that. They'll fly to a nearby perch, pluck feathers from prey, then rip it asunder and swallow.

If this happened and people watched, what would they think? Would they feel swelling anger, outraged at the murder they'd watched? Would they wish slow starvation for all Cooper's hawks so the world's every junco could live?

Maybe they would, because watching a junco die jolts the most hardened observer. It's violent, bloody—cold-blooded, you might say—except it keeps Cooper's hawks warm. Those who observe it must know the big picture, or one songbird's death will assume much too vital a role.

Would the people who watched see the beauty in hawks? Would they marvel at wildness and speed? Would they feel in their bones that the natural world provides juncos so raptors can eat?

No species of bird has ever become endangered because predators ate one too many. If people stay out of the way, nature keeps its own balance. Songbirds increase, and hawk numbers soon follow. Songbirds decline, and you won't see that hawk in your yard.

I don't enjoy films where my fellow men set out to stab, shoot or beat on each other. That is true violence, folks. It has nothing to do with a Cooper's hawk trying to live.

March

THE MOODIEST MONTH

March may be the muddiest, moodiest month of them all, but you can't help loving what it brings.

It's also the dustiest, dirtiest, brownest month ever devised. That still doesn't dampen the thrill of its coming.

For March strikes the match, lights the spark, guns the engine. It kindles a flame that can brighten your very tired eyes. It tells us we didn't stop tilting back there in December; we didn't get stuck faced away from the sun, doomed to cold winter nights for all time.

No, it's all working out like it does every year — at least that's what the mud and dust tell me.

It's interesting that March makes the best mud and dust, because these brownish media seem mutually exclusive. If there's mud, there's no dust, or so most months would have it, but March is a rebel of sorts.

In March it can rain for a week, making mud so back roads turn to slurry-filled swamps. Then the sun can come out, and the swamp can start baking. Things bubble. They ooze. Then they harden as moisture vacates. If a strong wind blows up, which it can during March, a tar pit can transform to dust within 48 hours.

So you drive through the country, aswirl in your self-made tornado. There's a truck up ahead, kicking clouds in your face, but who cares? There are geese overhead.

Above all the dirt, they course northward in Vs, teaming up with south winds to make human souls glad they're alive. The fact they do indicates how strong a spell they cast on us.

You know and I know, there aren't many times when one stops to make note that it feels great to breathe in and out. To their credit, geese force us to do this each year when the mud and dust season arrives.

It's hard to resist when the wind blows in zephyrs, stroking dry skin without slapping. It's hard to hold back when the geese fly so free, heeding dictates so old they were etched on the seasons when nature was all that there was.

Fog tends to heighten the stature of geese as primeval. They know where they're going, yet they can't see 10 feet, flapping through mush toward the spring. You squint up to see them — they're flying so low — hoping maybe a wedge will alight near your spot on the river.

Geese loom through the fog, necks extended, wings cupped, as they drop toward an island half-flooded by heavy March rains. Downward they drift, webbed feet pushed out in front, dropping softly toward muddy brown water.

They will rest for a day, preening feathers and honking while high pressure dissipates fog. With nightfall, they'll honk with a strange urgency — more high-pitched, more on edge with a tension only wanderlust can relieve.

Three slip from the trees, float downriver a moment, then run on the water toward flight. They lift off; a squadron on shore follows suit. It is dark, but the light from a full moon and Venus help human eyes track their progress.

Three or four times they will circle the island. Perhaps they are torn between staying and pushing ahead. But the timeless dictate conquers all on this night, and their voices fade off to the north.

Others will fly through the dark, with the moon on their shoulders. Songbirds will join them, and life will flow back to fill up winter's seasonal void. Next to geese through the fog, geese in front of the moon make the strongest spring statement of all.

How high they are flying is anyone's guess. But we know they are high — we all want to be with them — between Earth and the vastness of space.

HOOKED WHEN YOU LOOK IN THEIR EYES

To sit in a blind before dawn in mid-March is to pray spring will hurry along.

Cold finds new meaning before sun creeps over the mountain. This rings especially true if you're down in a hollow where midnight's worst chill seems to build on itself by degrees. God forbid there's a northwest wind whipping through leafless red maples. If so, it will cut like cold steel through your layers—wool, dacron and nylon that can't quite be feathers or fur.

Sure, it was worth it. A ruffed grouse walked by, nipping buds from a stand of young aspens. Skinny woodchucks strolled past, needing lunch and a female companion. Six deer sauntered through, never straying from cover, their eyes fixed on something (a blind) they had not seen before.

It could have been warm, though. The woods could have oozed with spring's balmy intentions; with sap flowing upward from roots toward the tops of the trees. I could have heard blackbirds chuck, chur overhead, or the honking of geese, but I didn't. Instead, winter cut me. It slashed me with cold. I stuck my face out the blind and the wind penetrated my bones.

No coffee, no book, no earphone radio with the news. Just the cold plunging deep through the sweat pants and wool, through the scarf and the snowmobile boots.

You shiver when that kind of cold has its way. You hunker your head down inside your coat collar, like a box turtle tucked in its shell. You blow in your gloves, ever softly so whitetails won't hear you. You pull your hat over your eyes and start hugging yourself.

None of it works. You are cramped and can't move. Fingertips start losing feel. Trees creak outside; no, they moan, they protest. It was 12 degrees when you left to come out here and freeze.

Resolve starts to crumble, eroding with each chilly minute. Coffee exists somewhere out of this woods. Warm-footed people are savoring civilized life. Outside your frail blind, brownish leaves kick along, the wind lifting them off frozen ground. No otters, no deer — only oodles of doubt as to whether you really are sane.

When the animals come, other problems arise. Making rapid adjustments, you touch tripod legs and metal camera bodies — barehanded, of course, because gloves are the tools of a bungler. You grab frigid lenses to focus on eyes; you place poor naked fingers on buttons and watch them turn blue.

All the while you are stiff as a board with pure tension. Wild things are so close you had better not breathe or they'll hear. To see through the lens, which is poked out a hole, you must bend down and stiffen your neck. Ten minutes of that, while you're holding your breath, and mild aches turn to throbbing discomfort.

It could have been warm while this torture transpired. I could have been sitting in shirtsleeves, with insects about. But you know something strange? I'll go back tomorrow. If you look in their eyes from that close, you get hooked. If you see every feather, and hear their feet walking, simple cold cannot keep you away.

A KODACHROME YEAR

Around they spin on a carousel, Kodachrome slides showing seasons that won't stay the same. The first frame shows early spring blackbirds; the last, pillowed ice on a deep winter stream. In between are 78 captured moments that document systems in flux.

If you had to cram your natural year into 80 quick flashes, which ones would your slide show project?

You might start with blackbirds. They herald the spring. Show males rising up from a half-frozen corn stubble field. Clouds of them waver past hillsides that hold back their green.

Below, on a flood plain, the river flows over its banks. Show streams rushing toward it. Show waterfalls gushing with runoff the aquifer needs. A picture of sap buckets fits in well here. Behind the big maples, cows lounge in the year's first warm sun.

As spring gains a foothold, show daffodils popping. Show willows all yellow; then farm fields plowed up as the crop year begins. Baby robins belong here. So do fawns with black noses that twitch.

Summer means tents and a fish fry or two. Perch fillets in a pan, at a lean-to, fit well. Loons yodel as campfires burn bright. Flash pictures of bullfrogs on spatterdock leaves; of turtles on logs, slipping off when your boat gets too close.

Woodchucks in gardens say "dog days" to some. Follow them with a beaver, its nose cutting Vs as dusk quiets a wilderness pond.

Autumn begins with thick fog after dawn. If you're sleeping outside, burrow down or your head will get cold. New England asters would fit well right here. Their purple seems deepest when glimpsed in a goldenrod field.

Chevrons of geese waver south against darkening skies. Show a buck with sharp antlers. Flash a picture of hoof prints in mud. Summer cabins are closed now. The river they watch flows past yards without children or noise.

When larch needles tumble, you must be prepared. Autumn's last embers have died.

Lest your audience figures the world's at an end, show snow on a crisp winter's day. Bird feeders brim over. Nuthatches get friendly again. After cross-country skiers say powdery prayers, they sink down in their beds as they would in drifts piled by the wind.

Show a picture of cottontail tracks in the snow, freshly stamped during pre-dawn patrols. Great horned owls are out prowling when rabbits gnaw shrubs. Owl eyes flashed on the screen say that nature is not always kind.

It's hard to believe, but you've run out of room. Your slots are all taken. Your natural year is defined. Show a hard-frozen stream, its bed covered by slick icy tiers. Winter's teeth have dug in, the year's come to a close.

Don't despair, though. Your carousel keeps right on spinning. The next slide shows springtime again.

GOODBYE TO FOREST GIANTS

I walked through an old quiet woodland recently. Forest giants lay dead all around me.

The monsters were beech trees, their gray trunks embedded in humus like elephants' feet. Some remained standing, all rotten and spongy, their cores gouged by woodpeckers looking for carpenter ants. Others lay strewn through the woods in a criss-crossing maze. Last week, or last year, a storm had blown through, wrenching their leafless skeletons from the soil and snapping them like straws in the wind. Behemoths had tumbled toward earth, branches flying. Monsters had slammed into dirt that would slowly absorb them.

It was eerie in there, far from road, far from people. It was me and those dead trees and thoughts about cycles and things.

The beeches were dead because fungi had killed them. The fungi's airborne spores had worked in consort with a species of scale insect, which bores into beech trees to siphon their sap. Tiny holes drilled by the insects had allowed fungal spores to invade the beech trees and kill them.

This has been going on for several decades: the systematic destruction of thousands and thousands of beech trees throughout the Northeast. Someday it will end, tree pathologists promise. A few genetically resistant beeches will survive to keep the species alive. The beech nuts they drop—and the saplings that result—will use that resistance to grow tall and strong, despite the fungal presence.

Someday, say the experts, giant beech trees will flourish again. Call me selfish, but I will be dirt then, and that makes me mad—for the beech tree is special.

To spend a lifetime walking through woodlands—and never pass through a cathedral of beeches—is to miss what the woods are about.

They're about beauty and feeding an army of wildlife. They're about helping people stay warm on a cold winter's night. The woods are about turkeys scratching in leaves; about putting your hand on a tree that feels smooth; about finding nuts inside burrs that you've broken apart.

An old beech is all these things; a deciduous monarch. Right now, the king's court lies in ruins.

Yes, there are bright sides. The woodpeckers think this is great. Dead beeches lure ants like comb honey attracts a black bear. Woodpeckers drill through the pith, eating ants left and right. When springtime arrives, the woodpeckers drill nest cavities in these same dying beeches. If they move out next year, flying squirrels or screech owls are shoo-ins to pick up the lease.

Woodcutters also find merit in lifeless beech wood. Since the fungus began wreaking havoc, they've been cutting, splitting and selling with smiles on their faces.

Beech trees make great firewood. Their wood burns forever, red-hot, crammed with foot-warming power. As beech trees have fallen, they have given their lives to make cordwood.

That's nice, but it doesn't put beeches back into the forest. It doesn't replace all the beechnuts that turkeys once ate or assure that a carpet of bronze leaves will carpet the woods every autumn.

Only time can make those promises; only decades passing, beech trees being forgotten and forests reworking themselves. Someday, in these forests, a kid with a jackknife will carve hearts in beechwood. Your kids and mine will know monarchs that day, when the forest grows giants again.

April

THE LION IS RISING

Orion is falling, the lion is rising and soon nighttime viewers will look for the sky dog and fail.

Stand out around midnight, and study the deep endless dark. With spring pressing forward, the night sky is changing. No longer does the constellation Orion stand watch over southern horizons. Instead, the great hunter sinks low in the west, his belt tarnished by night shine from shopping mall lights in the distance. Behind him the dog star, named Sirius, heels at his feet.

Our brightest night star, Sirius, burns bluish-white in the constellation Canis Major. It, too, will vacate the sky as the lion ascends.

Leo is the lion, a star constellation that climbs a sky perch every spring. Its huge curling head sits atop a lithe body, which sprawls from the east toward the south. Looking up at the lion, one sees pinpoints of light — stars requesting that viewers connect starry dots to see legs, manes and long, swishing tails.

That's easy to do on a sweet April night, with spring peepers and wood frogs in chorus. Wind soothes from the south, feeling tropical, soft. Skin absorbs moisture, shirt sleeves ripple gently; the mind knows that winter has gone.

If there were a moon, its bright face would reveal tiny bird silhouettes passing by. Legions of songbirds, avoiding skyscrapers, streak northward where insects abound; insects and space, where a bird can find food for a nestful of yammering mouths.

Why not fly northward at night in the spring, looking down at the bomb blasts of light radiating from cities? Why not follow snakes made by car lamps on highways that hug silt-clogged rivers in spate?

If I were a songbird, I'd fly north at night, knowing migrating hawks fly by day. At 500 feet, I'd be safe from all owls. They'd be hunting deer mice far below. At 1,000 feet, I would miss TV towers, those bird killers blinking their tiny red lights, telling airplanes to detour or die.

Far below, frogs called peepers would fill up balloons, swelling throat sacs to herald spring's coming. Amphibious signals would bounce off spike rushes. Wood frogs would join in, calling clackety-clack out of sync.

Waters would ripple, and frog skin would glisten, as slick and as shiny as arms on an old leather chair.

Once or twice I'd dip down if I saw a campfire, shooting sparks into black velvet space. I'd watch embers die and see orange reflections on faces that pressed toward the flames.

Only the righteous camp out before summer; I'd know these were true outdoor people. By getting out early, they have gained something precious: spring solitude, mixed with the frogs.

Maybe those people have fished through the day, wading streams, feeling legs numb with cold. Maybe they've hiked up a bugless high peak or canoed down a river that carried them easily, whisking them past craggy black willow trunks and their branch tips anointed with yellow.

Or maybe they worked at their jobs through the day, inside offices, factories, rooms without windows—where the air smelled like some old machine's inner workings and the thoughts were of conflict, of pressure, of goals gone unmet.

Maybe those people just had to escape—to camp under Leo's great mane. Maybe they figured they needed a cleansing; a flushing; a jolt that would recharge their world-weary spirits. If they did, they were right, because nothing puts trivia more in perspective than stars in a huge springtime sky.

SOMEBODY SLAP ME

Somebody slap me. I'm starting to think about keeping a goat on the place. Or maybe some sheep, or some geese. And why not a super-sized Quonset hut greenhouse? I need one for vegetables, houseplants and seedlings.

And heaps of manure—piles of it composting, rotting toward black gold that crumbles between my fingers.

And mules for the plow and a half-acre corn field. And maybe a barn, so the creatures have someplace to live.

Somebody slap me, then keep me away from those organic farmer-type people. It's their fault, acting so friendly, showing me simplified lives, infiltrating my thoughts with this business of small-scale agriculture, living off the land, producing your own food. Before you know it, I'm going to start believing it's possible to live in the United States without being chewed up by the need for possessions.

I'm going to start realizing it's possible to live harmoniously with nature without getting caught in a nerved-up, pressure-packed, unfulfilling lifestyle that seems bent on this green earth's destruction.

Those organic farmers are crafty. The ones I've met don't make a big thing of the fact they've found something good. They just live their lives, learning how to build things from natural materials, fix things that break and make enough money growing crops and raising livestock so their lives can go on in this manner.

I've visited three such families recently. They share a number of characteristics.

All are intelligent. None are originally farmers. Isn't that interesting? They could have done other things, gotten "good" jobs, flowed smoothly into the cultural mainstream. Instead, they chose lives they knew would never make them rich.

They enjoy physical work. They enjoy animals, fresh air and living so close to the seasonal flow they can feel every beat of its pulse. They figure chemicals don't help a farmer, so they shun them for natural fertilizers, natural livestock feed, natural food for themselves. They figure if everyone did this, planet Earth would begin healing fast. Interesting.

They seem inquisitive, ready to ask how you did something they'd like to learn. They read a lot but own few televisions. For the most part, their vehicles are old, kept going by the knowledge of what engines need to survive.

They're not hermits. They keep tuned to events, although the news on the ecological front tends to discourage them. They participate in community events, especially those where they can share their knowledge and learn skills from like-minded people.

They enjoy shared community labor. They wish there were more barn raisings, more rural community centers, more places where goat folks could meet up with sheep folks and knitters could sit down with quilters.

Somehow they've focused on natural things: making food from the land, making fuel from its trees, making clothes from the wool of its creatures.

None are rich. None want to be, if wealth means forsaking the ground rules they've set for themselves. None are poor, either.

Financially speaking, they minimize expenses and keep their bills paid. Spiritually speaking, they seem well-to-do. They are not having breakdowns. Their medicine chests do not bristle with drugs for their tension. They have traded off one set of goals for another. In their view, it simply makes sense.

So bring on the goats, the mules and manure. These organic people have made a convert. If you meet them, they'll make you look inward and question. What path are you on? What life goals have you set? What would happen if these were to change?

THE PLACES WE'VE BEEN

I've thought of the places we've been these past years, you and me and my dingy brown truck. I've concluded I'm glad I could share all these places with you.

Let's harken back; let's recap our past triumphs. I suppose we should dwell on a few awesome failures as well. Without you, good reader, I wouldn't have found myself jouncing through potholes the size of some small Eastern states. Without your inspiration I wouldn't have locked myself out of the truck on a road no one else knew existed.

Ah, the places we went; all the coffee we sipped while our eyes scanned the hillsides for birds. I can't count all the times we set out in the snow to watch rough-legged hawks over fields. Farmland in winter seems frigid, forboding. It does until rough-legged hawks drop from trees, skimming low, wings extended, eyes flashing with hungry intent.

Every once in awhile, I'm quite sure you'll remember, winter fields also yielded horned larks in manure or a turkey flock crossing a road, caught betwixt and between.

On the coldest of days starling hordes flocked toward thick heaps of silage. They combed it like ants on an overripe honeydew melon. Warmer days told cock pheasants the world needed seeing. We watched as they tiptoed from hedgerow hangouts and proceeded to pick through the corn.

And of course there were ducks. We have chewed up more time watching them than I'd care to remember. Wars have started and ended while our field glasses soaked in mergansers. In the afternoon sun, with the marsh shouting spring, males would fan their white crests and we'd gasp.

Here's a wet little spot where we always find mallards. What? There aren't any here? So I goofed; Mr. Nature ain't perfect. Overhead—what are those? They are common mergansers, necks extended like feathered stilettos. Here come black ducks; just look for their white underwings. There go mallards; the female is quacking.

We have stood at a beaver pond deep in the twilight and watched wood ducks returning to roost. They appeared as black dots on the western horizon, silhouetted against watercolor-like streaks of magenta.

In an instant their shapes whistled past us like missiles—the friendliest kind, stuffed with acorns and ready for sleep. Then they put on the brakes, banked quick left, then quick right, carving figures in air like a skater might do on the ice. With soft plops they landed, then ripples subsided. Heron croaks told us night had descended.

We have walked up steep gorges and paddled canoes, me with notebook in hand, mind wheels turning to find the right word. Didn't I write about it when you darned near capsized me? Or was that me that lurched sideways when the beaver tail crashed on the water not five feet away? All I know is I swore quite a bit when it happened. Mr. Nature ain't perfect, you know.

We've looked up at hemlocks that swayed overhead. We have looked down at tumbling water. We have felt wind so raw that it made us gush tears and felt sun blazing hot with the summer. As for dust, I feel sorry for walking you through it. It was March, after all, and the marsh grass was dirty and rains hadn't freshened the earth.

But that's how we got all those stories, good reader. You said, "Get out there!" and I needed you for a friend.

The way this guy sees it, we've made a blood oath: to drink deeply of what counts in life. Forget the great American novel. I'll write it next time when the indoor life beckons more strongly.

In this life, however, we're bound to get muddy. I pray we'll see wood ducks for many more years down the line.

WHAT THE WIND GIVES
(AND THEN TAKES AWAY)

The south wind gives, and the south wind takes away.

Spring finds it giving us ducks on the wing, migrant fliers enamored of tailwinds. Three days later, if it blows once again, it may well take these birds farther north.

People attuned to how spring ought to feel know that sensing a south wind is vital. Through study they've learned April's waterfowl lesson: that those sensing such breezes see ducks. Honing their skills every year at this time, they can sniff a south breeze before hints of it brush past their faces.

Perhaps these people sense imperceptible rises in humidity. Perhaps their inner ears tell them there's been a change in barometric pressure. Whatever their tricks, they need only face south, take a sniff and stare up at the sky. If it's coming, they'll smile, then dash inside for bird books and car keys.

The rest of us know when white pine boughs bend back and the wind doesn't bite like it used to. By the time we've arrived at our favorite wetland, waves are rippling its waters to signal a south wind.

A fortnight of north wind has created a logjam of ducks many miles to the south. Scaup have backed up on the vast Chesapeake; mallards have stalled, marking time, on the Delaware Bay. Now the wind has released them to gush north with instinctive purpose.

Three pairs of mallards make Vs through the shallows, their bills plucking at spears of new grass. A twig snaps on shore, causing necks on the drakes to stretch high, like they've gained vertebrae. Then the heads start to swivel as ducks try to sense if there's danger.

Beyond them, in muck that would suck off your shoes, blue-winged teal search for tuberous roots. For birds puddling in ooze, their heads buried in mud, they maintain a demeanor of grace.

There are eight; all are paired—the four drakes showing white facial crescents. Something spooks them; they leap up, their wings beating madly. In seconds they've cleared distant trees.

Moments later, they're back, cupping wings that show powder-blue patches. With wings set and webbed landing gear dangling down, they alight with the softest of splashes.

Other birds take their place in a blue, clearing sky, flying north up a broad river channel. There are four, close together; two have red bills and feet. All have bodies that taper like knives. They are common mergansers, their bills notched like saws so that minnows cannot slip away.

The males are the bright ones: blood-red beaks, emerald heads and snow white on their bellies.

Below them, a mixed flock of wood ducks and green-winged teal leap from a swale thick with food. The teal drakes show rust on their heads and bright green on their wings. Staying low to the water, they depart like small rockets, their fuel being duckweed and such.

Like their blue-winged soul mates, they bank sharply and circle. Then they drop on set wings, homing in on the swale where they find the shoots tender and new. Something stops them, however. Only 10 feet from touch down, they flare, catch the wind and are gone.

Great blue herons flap slowly toward boggy hideouts, their legs trailing behind like bent straws. Above them, an osprey's bent wings carve tight circles.

The hovering bird looks straight down. In the shallows below no carp makes a false move, so the beautiful fish hawk moves north.

So will the others if winds remain strong—all the teal, the mergansers, the scaup. The mallards might stay, though; the wood ducks as well. The south wind may have blown them back home.

May

COLD SNAKE, WARM FINGERS

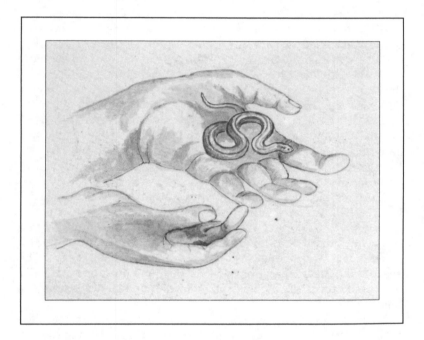

There's one good thing about clearing rocks for a garden: It allows one to meet friendly snakes.

I always pick rocks with gloves on, just in case the snakes I uncover haven't heard how nice I am. A snoozing water snake, for example, doesn't react well to having its roof ripped away. Even a garter snake—friendly to a fault under most circumstances—will react defensively to such an intrusion.

But there's one snake that never strikes out when discovered; one snake I handle without gloves whenever I can. It's the red-bellied snake—docile, charming, a joy to behold. Lock me in a room with a red-bellied snake and a person who fears all reptiles, and I'll still give you odds I can change how that person views snakes.

My daughter doesn't need changing. She's 7 and hasn't acquired "the fear." Every time I'm picking rocks, turn one over and uncover a red-bellied snake, I call her over. She's usually nearby—in dirt, mud or water—constructing whole worlds in her mind.

If the day is a cool one in spring, the snake will not move very quickly. My hand reaches down, lifts a rock and reveals it, coiled still like a thin strand of rope. Pale brown on the top, looking dusty like last year's dead leaves, it measures 8 inches long and is not as thick as your little finger. Slowly its tongue flicks out as it smells. Off come my gloves because now I crave tactile contact.

The first treat is color, a blast of bright orange that runs down the snake's smooth-scaled belly. Gently I pick up the reptile and gaze at its bright underside. The belly surface is flat, not rounded like the rest of its body. Smooth to the touch, it is totally dry. Scales cover its length, overlapping seamlessly every quarter inch or so.

The cold-blooded snake finds my warm-blooded hands like a blanket. The longer I hold it, the more it thinks moving is fun. It doesn't try to flee or bite, however; it just winds through my fingers, like a vine tendril weaves through a trellis.

The child has arrived, hands out-stretched, looking eager. This snake's reputation has preceded it. If you've met one red-belly, you've met them all. She holds it, admires it and guides it from one hand to the next.

Does she know that snakes do not have ears and use tongues as their sniffers? She does. Does she know that those sporting red bellies give birth to a dozen live young? She doesn't and presses for more information.

How big are the babies? They're 4 inches long. Do they stay with their mother? They don't; they must fend for themselves, eating slugs and small insects, from the moment they touch the good earth.

Her friend has warmed up now. It slides through her fingers, defying all friction. Perhaps, I suggest, we should put the snake down. Yes, we should, she concurs, while detente is the word of the day.

It isn't much of a liberation. The red-bellied snake slinks three feet to a stump, crawls atop it and coils for a nap. "Let's pick some more rocks," says the kid, eyes aglitter. With luck, she'll locate one more snake.

MAN SHOT WATCHING GRACKLES

I never met a grackle that was worth getting shot at to see.

An ivory-billed woodpecker? Definitely. A grackle? You've got to be kidding.

But life throws some curveballs, and so it was, on a beautiful spring morning—with tree swallows dipping overhead and the air sweet with crab apple fragrance—a lady, a gun and my craving for grackles converged.

She was a nice lady, and, it must be said, she kept the Smith and Wesson .38 special in its holster throughout our conversation. But she was holding it by the grip and we were alone in the boondocks, and I had, after all, appeared at her home unannounced.

Honest, ma'am, I just came to see grackles. They're up at the beaver pond behind the house. Your husband knows me, remember? I met you last week when he invited me up to admire the duck boxes he'd built.

Her grip on the gun softened. She smiled. She remembered. My pitiful life had been spared.

I couldn't blame her, really. Her husband was away at work, and they'd been broken into twice within the past two months. I had tried to call, but she'd been out at the store. When I got there, I had knocked on the door. She couldn't see my truck from the upstairs window, so she figured she'd better be safe.

I got some milk and a brownie after she found out I wasn't a burglar. Then she sent me off toward the beaver pond, there to ponder the fragility of life and the beauty of grackles.

They are gorgeous, the males of the species. Slightly larger and more streamlined than robins, with long wedge-shaped tails, these "crow blackbirds" appear uniformily black at a distance. But creep closer; look harder.

In the spring, each one's head shines with metallic reflections of peacock blue and purple. Amid all this blue is a bright yellow eye, just as bold as a hawk's or an eagle's. Below, on the body, bronze feathers catch sun rays. The sheen that results makes one think of sunlight on old brass.

All is not gorgeous about grackles, however. They sing with a loud metallic squeak, more like a rusty hinge than a song. Also, they are nest robbers and crop eaters, which makes them unpopular with people who like birds to behave like good people.

At the beaver pond, only their good traits prevailed. First of all, I never knew grackles were so good at spearing things in the water. Time and again, I watched as they skulked amid sedges, spearing aquatic insects with all the aplomb of green herons.

Their greatest moments, however, occurred when they burst into song. Actually, it was not in the singing, but in the building up to it, that the grackles proved so captivating.

The ritual followed strict guidelines. Perched on a low branch or atop a clump of rushes, a male grackle initiated his preamble to song by slowly puffing out his plumage. As his feathers expanded, he began partially extending his wings and spreading his tail.

Slowly he puffed and extended and spread, growing rounder with each passing second. Just when I thought he would burst, he let loose with a squeak. It was very anti-climactic, but that's what it was. Then he deflated, like a hat pin had popped his balloon.

Much ado about nothing, I guess you could say. Grackles talk a good game; then they squeak. But the females respond, and the grackle world thrives, so the system works just as it should.

You might think that wood ducks would be more exciting. A drake swam 10 feet from my blind in the sunlight that morning. You might think three deer wading up to their bellies, their mouths filled with aquatic plants, would be best. Or the red-shouldered hawk that flew over. Or the hooded merganser female swimming through a maze of dead snags.

Or even the spotted sandpiper skittering along a semi-submerged log, its rear end twitching up and then down.

But the grackles were tops, several feet from my nose, puffing up, making squeaks, catching bugs.

Come to think of it, maybe they were worth a bullet or two. It was a beautiful day, the pond setting was perfect and the sun on their plumage was striking. "Man shot watching grackles" the head-line would read. Something tells me I'd make the front page.

DON'T SHRINK FROM THIS CREATURE

Fortunate is the person who can find a spotted salamander one day and its slimy egg masses the next—fortunate and hard-working, that is.

To enjoy such good luck, a naturalist must not only be lucky, he or she must pay dues by venturing afield as frequently as possible. Only by repeated forays down damp woodland paths and along the edges of algae-filled ponds will the odds of experiencing salamander goodness reach reasonable proportions.

Does a "good salamander" imply contradiction? Is a salamander loathesome and slippery, too disgusting to touch, filled with venom and poised for attack?

Many people used to think do, but these are enlightened times. Most modern humans know salamanders are toothless, harmless creatures that have to stay moist, because dry skin means death to their kind. Like all amphibians, they must keep their skin damp to avoid desiccation; so too must their eggs remain shielded from sunlight and wind.

Eggs are the reason they migrate to water each spring. Unlike those of reptiles and birds, an amphibian's eggs don't come with a shell-like outer covering. Instead, they are soft and jelly-like and must be deposited in water to avoid drying out.

Although many amphibians, such as the spotted salamander, live on land, they must return to the water each spring to produce their offspring. There is poetic justice is this annual trek, because millions of years ago, salamanders emerged from the water, evolving from gilled aquatic creatures. Their vernal return is a homecoming of sorts, an affirmation of aqueous roots.

When spring comes and spotted slamanders leave their forest homes in search of shallow breeding ponds, that's when you see them on paths. Other times of year, you hardly ever see them because they hide under leaves to keep moist and find earthworms to eat. After they have laid their eggs, you can find their gelatinous egg clusters floating suspended in 5 or 6 inches of water. These clusters often contain up to 200 pea-sized eggs, encased in a jelly-like blob that can be 6 inches long and 4 inches across.

When the eggs are first laid, the salamanders resemble black dots inside their jelly spheres. Three weeks later they hatch into half-inch-long larvae that transform into adults about three months later when they reach 3 inches long.

Sadly, that's all the time we have for natural history. We need to discuss gut reactions.

How would you react if you came upon a spotted salamander? Remember, an adult is 7 inches long, with moist features and soft skin; the body feels like it is boneless, perhaps made from Jell-O. Large yellow spots brighten a coal-black body. Its overall aura is distinctly primitive; a throwback to times when most creatures on earth shrank from sunlight for fear it would kill them.

Let's hope you wouldn't throw a snake fit if you saw one. Talk about primitive — that kind of irrational, instinctive revulsion is the hardest to calm of all fears.

Let's hope you would photograph, ogle, then return it to the water. Let's hope you would wonder, ask questions and feel part of burgeoning spring.

Only the fortunate get to see salamanders. Don your boots and seek them before eggs hatch and summer begins.

KIDS IN THE FOREST

American kids move quite fast in the forest. One minute you see them; the next they've dashed clean out of sight—unless, of course, they're bored, in which case they sit on their rear ends and pout.

Both the speedy and the torpid graced me with their presence on a recent sashay through the woods. They had the look of fifth graders—a gangly strain, mostly—all elbows, knob knees and big feet. Like puppies on leashes, they strained to run free as we entered a cool, shady woodland. Feeling old, like the forest, I poked along finding things, constantly holding them back.

I talked quite a bit while they tried not to listen. My mouth issued forth an incessant blather of facts. What would intrigue them, these urban rapscallions? After three separate walks, I can tell you it wasn't club moss.

They liked birds' nests, though, and salamanders. They liked mud, dirt and rocks. If a rock lay flat, they turned it over. In the process, earthworms were uncovered; hordes of black ants raced about. The kids paid attention while all this transpired, as opposed to the times when I droned about ferns—or the difference between oaks and maples.

They also liked animals, signs of animals or abodes built by animals. A set of raccoon tracks in mud slowed them down for a full 30 seconds. So did an impressively gnawed oak tree, its trunk set upon by a beaver. As for abodes, we found birds' nests galore— some with eggs, some half-built, some abandoned.

Kids like to grab things like nests, so restraint was in order. "Keep your hands off that nest!" I screamed out, and sometimes it would work. No damage was done. The robins and phoebes we traumatized should bounce back soon.

Kids have sharp eyes; there's no doubt about that. As soon as I said, "Find some birds," they were pointing them out. One youth (identified as a future Thoreau by his unlaced sneakers and Los Angeles Raiders jacket) spied a woodpecker and knew what it was.

His cohorts derived brief, but genuine, pleasure in learning it sucked sap from trees. Another kid noted a flycatcher perched high above us. The wood peewee dashed out and snapped up a bug on the wing.

We moved down the trail like a street sweeper does, leaving all sorts of dust in our wake. In the process, chipmunks squeaked and ran for cover, birds clucked flustered retreats and flowers prayed shoes wouldn't stomp them.

When we did stop, it always revolved around water, which pulls on youngsters like a magnet.

If you sit in the woods watching kids splash in streams, you'll remember what that age was like. It was wanting to run everywhere at the same time, never knowing quite what you would find. When you came upon something—a toad or a squirrel—you just liked it; its name didn't matter.

Life was near-freedom. Your mind was still open; you would take off your shoes in a flash. Every stream promised crayfish, and puddles held polywog swarms.

What did I think as we barged through the forest? I'll remember those bare feet, while kids looked for crayfish, feeling pleasure that needed no name.

June

CHANGE AND THE RIVER

Nature means change, only some things change faster than others.

Birds molt winter plumage to gain breeding feathers, but this can take weeks to accomplish. Deer coats transform from ash gray to rich brown, but it doesn't occur in an hour. Only rivers and skies seem to relish the fact they can alter their moods overnight.

Rivers use rain to effect their makeover. Thunder rolls from the west in the night, shaking windows. By morning, smooth glides churn a thick muddy brown, clogged with flotsam from neighboring fields. Yesterday's river slipped slowly, deep green. Today it will kill those who think they can go for a ride.

Knowing how quickly a river can change, we should relish sweet moments upon one. Not only can storms turn a river unfriendly, but people can show up in droves and that changes the mood. There's a place in this world for the raucous tube floaters, their shouts ricocheting downstream — it's just not my place. My place on a river is quiet, so quiet that voices a half-mile upwind perk my ears as they skim over water.

I like to hear rivers flowing, their molecules sliding like glass over boulders, their wavelets slip-slapping against me when breezes blow up. I enjoy hearing ostrich fern fronds on their banks waving backwards and forwards, so jungle-like, verdant and fresh. I relish the sipping sound big trout often make when they inhale a surface mayfly.

That's my kind of river — the one that hypnotizes, transfixes, relaxes, inspires with its seemingly eternal flow.

One shouldn't just listen, of course, one should look. The two go together; they're born of the same mental outlook. One who strains to hear gurgles will strain to make out what that yellow bird is, the one perched over there in that bush. It's a yellow warbler, much brighter than butter.

The warbler's home roost is a riverbank thick with tall grasses. Ferns fight for space here. Sycamore trees rise above the turf battle, as do vultures that float overhead on air pillows, their wings getting something for nothing. Back on the ground, the air vibrates with bird songs. It's a charge you can feel, a life current of whistles and trills.

You want to count birds? You can do it here; get out your book. Scribble down hummingbird, oriole, redstart, phoebe. Take a breath, scribble more — names like yellowthroat, kingbird, kingfisher.

Take a break, look upriver. A twilight deer crossing transpires. Their coats are so red at this time of the year. Their forelegs churn foam as they slice through the riffles. Splashing ashore, the deer hit the tall grass, which absorbs them the way sand blots raindrops.

Soon bats will emerge as the night river starts taking over. Sounds will become even more magnified as the mind starts to play little games. What was that splash over there in the shallows? A beaver? A gremlin? A troll? Watch out for smooth rocks hiding under the surface. They will wrench you from lethargy, then send you sprawling face first.

Darkness descends. There's a friend out there somewhere, a warm human body that talks. He gave you some space before dark, walking off down the river. Now you call out. He appears, walking softly, his cotton shirt soft like thick air that hangs over the river.

The two of you walk, splashing softly, toward home. Rivers change, but not that fast. Tonight, anyway, rain is far to the west. Trout will sip softly and water won't rush anywhere.

SPARE THAT TREE FOR A FALCON

Hubby had his chain saw out. That dead tree had to go.

The darned thing nearly blew over during last night's thunderstorm. With its bark peeling off and its leafless branches jutting out like snapped spears, the sugar maple had groaned so loudly during one gust that everyone ran to the basement.

Decades ago, a farmer had planted this maple along the driveway in hopes it would yield maple syrup. No doubt it complied, but those halcyon days were long gone. Now the old tree was a menace, an eyesore. It would fall to the chain saw come morning.

It didn't, however. A pair of swift-flying falcons called kestrels intervened by revealing their nest in the tree.

Nature constructed the nest, actually. As age took its toll, a branch had broken from the maple about 10 feet above ground. A knothole had formed where the branch broke away. Earlier in the spring, the kestrels had found it and claimed it as home.

High over hay fields that bordered the house, the male had courted his mate by executing a series of deep dives and upward swoops over the nest area. His wings beating deeply during each of these dives, the male had cemented the pair bond by bringing mice and insects to a special feeding perch, where the female accepted his gifts.

Soon afterward, the female had laid a single egg at the bottom of the cavity in the old maple. During incubation, she had left the nest for only four hours a day, to preen and eat food the male had captured for her. During that time, the male had replaced her in the cavity.

This changing of the guard had taken place in a flash—the male zooming in, stopping momentarily at the cavity opening, then disappearing deep in the hole. A split-second later, the female popped out, glanced about and took off at full speed.

Not 20 feet away, in the house with the chain saw, a human pair raised little kids. Falcons around? Soaring hunters nearby? No one knew birds were around.

The kestrel chick hatched, then sat under its mother, while the male hunted food in the fields. The male brought food to the nest twice a day—in and out, very quickly. The humans saw nothing; the young kestrel grew by the day.

After three weeks, however, the young bird got antsy. Its wings needed stretching. The world needed seeing. An urge pushed it up toward the light.

One night a storm came. Wind whipped across hay fields; it sawed the old tree back and forth. The next morning a bird's head appeared in the knothole. A kestrel climbed up to the edge of the hole, perched upon it and fluttered its wings.

The chain saw brigade witnessed this and stopped dead in its tracks. Great excitement ensued. A camera appeared. Like magic, that lousy old tree had become something worthy of note.

The young bird left home several days after that. The old sugar maple still stands. Concerned for his house, the saw owner will soon cut it down. In the spirit of compromise, however, he'll cut out a section that contains the knothole and then wire the whole section to a maple that's standing nearby.

What will happen next year, when the kestrels return? Will they pick the old knothole again? Stay tuned, falcon lovers. That old maple isn't dead yet.

STRIPPING VENEER

People change when they camp out and sleep on the ground in the woods. They stop being fuddy-duddies. They also stop changing their socks.

In the long run, it's better to spend time with a real person in old socks than a conceited person in clean ones. That's why I recommend gathering a dozen or so friends together and going on a tenting excursion. In addition to friends, take a few folks you don't know too well but whose vibrations please you. Two days in a tent, and you'll know if they warrant your trust.

The whole camping experience rejects aloofness and shrivels inflated egos. First of all, no one looks very good on the trail. One day in the rain, and your coiffure goes right out the window. Beards sprout on men. Women start wearing baseball caps — and not taking them off. Instead of some musk for the singles bar set, everyone lathers on bug repellent. Eau de insect—it's the ultimate turn-on. The jet set will sniff it out soon.

As for on-the-trail fashion, the same shirts get pulled out for days at a time, while the same jeans suffer knee hole enlargement. People sit on the ground, wipe their hands on their pants and negotiate mud holes in sneakers.

And work—let's talk work. There are jobs to be done, most of which tend to fall short on glamour. Pots always need scrubbing, tents always need pitching, potatoes will not skin themselves. Someone has to collect firewood; someone has to string a clothesline. People must cook food while clouds of wood smoke fill their eyes.

It's a jungle out there for a person who cannot act human. The world of woods camping strips off all veneers. It separates the wheat of true friendship from the chaff of small talk and pretense.

When the friendship shines through, it breaks down inhibition. People who think of themselves as reserved end up bellowing Mitch Miller tunes. Others start bringing up things they once thought were big secrets.

Stupid jokes get told. Deep feelings find expression. Giddiness mixes with heartfelt emotion in a blend you won't find at the office.

At night, it gets cold; people sleep in their clothes, bundled deep within fabric cocoons. Stacked four to a tent, they are unisex lumps—some as quiet as mice, others sawing the softest of logs.

If you don't go to sleep right away, you can ponder what all of this means. Why do people act so artificial in buildings and so real outdoors? For one thing, people indoors can't hear rain on a tent roof at night. They can't push a flap back the next morning and watch sunlight beams slant through dense fog. They can't hike or canoe all day, eat anything in sight anytime they want and not gain an ounce in a week.

They can't concentrate fully on birds, trees and rivers; on blending with nature, not beating it back with a stick.

Perhaps it's that simple: People in tents want to be friends with nature. Nature rewards them by letting them feel like themselves.

WHERE THE TREES KNOW YOUR NAME

Find a globe, spin it fast, close your eyes, stab a spot with your finger. What place have you found? Is it better than home? Are the bird colors brighter, the breezes more soothing, the people more tuned to the earth?

They might seem to be, because beauty enwraps our small world. For every ravaged rain forest and oil-fouled harbor, there's a spot where you still can wake up and think nature has won.

Some folks leave home and explore in the tropics, where the wind rattles palm fronds and ceiling fans whir through the night. Canoeing through mangroves, they watch for iguanas that lie flat on branches and let their long tails swing like vines. These travelers stop in small villages, scatter chickens, and ask for a small bite to eat. Sweat rolls off their noses as they sit in tin-roofed jungle houses, eating stewed cashew fruits spread like prune whip on good bread.

Eschewing the jungle, other people leave home to dive deep among coral fan forests. Above them, waves roll from the sea, hit a barrier reef, then form curls that shine green in the sun. In the water below, schools of tropical fish sway as one to the beat of the tide.

Still other folks wait until summer's heat sizzles. Then they head north toward conifer forests. Does a cool northern forest smell better than yours? Does it rank at the top, with its evergreen perfume, the kind you smell best when it rains?

You'll think that it does while your feet tread on needles as soft underfoot as a dark, spongy layer of peat. You'll start thinking cool northern air is the best in the world.

Maybe you'll leave home and go to Nebraska, to watch sandhill cranes on the wing. Maybe you'll climb up the Rockies in winter, where purplish jays scream from blue spruces laden with snow. Are purplish jays any better than blue ones? Is a mountain range better if its spines are more jagged; if its peaks seem raw and young in the ancient scheme of wind, rain and time?

For the moment they might be, but just get me home. There may not be 15 species of hummingbirds at home — there's just one — but I know where it perches and just how the sun hits its throat. I can sit in the evening and watch it from a chair I'm not paying for by the day or the week. No guide has to show me the blue of its wings while it hovers and sips with its tongue.

I like my hills, too, even though they're worn down, ground to soft undulations by time. I like my wrens and my black-and-white warbler; every day I can count on their songs.

I like home; it's my place. All the trees know my name. When it's humid, I turn on the fan. Someone else's iguana is my eft salamander, bright orange and soft in the forest. Someone else's toucan is my cardinal, my jay. Someone's breadfruit is my shiny apple.

See the world, soak it in, then come back home and open your eyes. You'll like what you see in your very green place. It's your world. It's your forest. It's home.

July

THEY STRIKE WHILE YOU'RE SLEEPING

It's quiet around the old homestead — too quiet.

Where are the pests — winged, toothed and sharp-clawed — who have plagued me on summer days passed? Where are the garbage can raiders, lawn gougers, leaf chewers? Whither the vegetable eaters I love?

They're holding back, waiting for a false sense of security to anesthesize my normally keen senses. They're waiting for me to put the guns away, bury the chemicals and take down every strand of barbed wire.

Then they'll strike, while I'm sleeping. The sound of teeth grinding will bolt me upright. They'll be out there—ripping and tearing and laughing at how they one-upped me.

That's what they think. The truth is I've kept my guard up.

Alertness did start to wane around the Fourth of July. By that time, woodchuck guerillas should have conducted their first spying missions. This year, however, no plump furtive shapes crept through weeds as they checked out the garden. There hadn't been any deer, either, their molars pre-sharpened to grind pretty flowers to mush.

And where were the skunks? Every morning I'd go out, expecting to find the lawn pockmarked by golfball-sized craters. Weren't there Japanese beetle larvae in the sod this year? Would the little skunks starve if this food source was taken away?

Even the gypsy moths seemed to be staying away. On oak hills around me, they'd chewed every leaf until branches stood out like scarecrows. In my little forest, they'd stopped short of that. Sure, there were caterpillars around—spiny, ugly, eating machines—but I had to listen hard to hear their mandibles chomping. Some of my friends could remove them from trees by the bushel. I had to settle for singles or clusters of three.

So that's how a lack of aggression by pests began lulling me falsely to sleep. After all, I have written glowingly about creatures for many moons now. Maybe word had seeped out: Give that nice Mr. Nature a break.

Hah! Anyone foolish enough to buy that doesn't know how freeloaders do business.

First came the raccoons, a fortnight ago. They slurped all the nectar from the hummingbird feeder, then knocked over three garbage cans. Three little ones trailed behind their big fat mother. I shouted, but none of them blinked.

Then came the deer—five at once in the morning: two bucks in their velvet, twin fawns and a doe. Just the night before I'd finally stopped spraying the perennials with a repugnant concoction that smelled like ammonia and rotten eggs. Now, just like vultures, they hovered about: Bambi's mother and four hangers-on.

"Come look at the fawns," I instructed the kids. They were darling, I had to admit. When one of them stepped toward the garden, however, I ran out the back door in full battle cry, shrieking wildly and flailing my arms.

They ran, which relieved me. How long they'll be gone I can't say.

Meanwhile, in the yard, a slow buzzing consumes me. Japanese beetles, insatiably hungry, are winging their way toward the roses.

What's that noise in the trees? Gypsy moths have regrouped. Now they're chewing with reckless abandon. A woodchuck ate all of the peppers last Sunday—dug under the fence and went wild.

The skunks are the only ones left. They should be back next week. One could spray me, I guess. That would launch the pest season with flair.

ODE TO A DEAD MOUSE

Chris, a good friend, had a mouse die in his truck. It was a white-footed mouse, and we grieved.

White-footed mice are a beautiful lot. Blessed with black shiny eyes and the softest brown fur, they scurry about under leaves in the forest, eating seeds, fruits and numerous insects. Hardly anyone I know would want to kill one, especially Chris, who likes mice. But this critter did itself in.

The problem is: Mice can be curious. This one managed to scurry into the cab of a pickup truck parked in the woods. The windows were open, but who knows why it skittered inside?

Maybe someone dropped part of a peanut butter sandwich on the floor of the cab, and it got pushed under the seat. Maybe the mouse sniffed it out and was munching contentedly when Chris opened the door and discovered it.

We'll never know, because the mouse, seeing Chris, ran up under the seat and was gone. "He found his way in." Chris decided. "I'll bet he can find his way out."

Case closed; life went on. My friend drove to and fro for the next several days, thinking nothing of white-footed mice. On one of those days—an especially hot one—he drove into town, parked and rolled all the windows up tight. Boy, was it hot in the cab when he came back. It smelled different, too, like it does in the heat when things die.

Chris knew what had happened. He felt great remorse. At the very least, the dead mouse deserved a decent burial. But where was the deceased? While its fragrance pervaded the cab's atmosphere, its remnants were not to be found.

Chris looked under the seats, searched behind the dashboard, even emptied the glove box of maps. Nothing—no mouse—just a bouquet of death that prevented his shutting the windows.

That was a week back—and still no solution. We're waiting to see just how long the aroma will last. Chris has taken to driving everywhere with the windows wide open and the fan blasting air. His passengers have adapted by riding around like dogs do on hot summer days: with their heads hanging out of the window.

Which brings me to Queen Anne's lace, the silver lining in all this. Driving along back roads, in July, with one's head out a window, one can drink in a Queen Anne's bouquet. Sure, they are weeds, these invaders of roadsides and ditches. But they're beautiful, too, with their flattened white heads nodding gently in lacy profusion.

They're peaking right now, I can say with authority. Last Sunday the mouse murderer gave me a call. "I just bought a buzz saw. Let's go pick it up." It was heavy; he needed help lifting.

So we motored from one country spot to another, my head out the window while flower smells blew in my face. I pretended I was a golden retriever, my tongue hanging down while I inhaled the breeze with great gulps.

Thousands of Queen Anne's lace flowers whizzed by. Mice notwithstanding, this summer day smelled like a million.

BIRDING IN BOVINE ENVIRONS

With summer upon us, and cows everywhere, let's review the three basic rules of birding in bovine environs. Rule 1: Avoid sharing space with a herd of beef cows. Rule 2: When walking where said herd has wandered, wear shoes you don't care much about. Rule 3: Be careful with barbed wire. It's two inches higher than you think before lifting your leg to climb over.

These rules sound simple, conceptually. "Just use common sense," most smart readers would say.

That's fine until the pressure's on. That's okay for namby-pamby birders who feel they must plan every trip in detail, review potential pitfalls in advance, then tote tons of gear that can meet every challenge.

But that's not me, folks, and that's not you. We're birding free spirits. We grab for the gusto no matter what kind of shoes we've got on. If opportunity knocks, we crash through the door. Let the timid procrastinate. To the bold go bright birds of a lifetime.

You're hesitating, I can feel it. Some strange sense of order balks at rushing, unready, toward cow pies and wire. The wild side beckons, but you're not sure you've got what it takes. To help you decide, I offer the following scenario. It's based on a true-life adventure that unfolded recently in the domain of the upstate New York dairy princess. If you relate to the hero, you're one of the bold. If you don't, you can go take a hike.

Brrring. . .brrring. Your phone is ringing. It's mom. She's got her bird voice cranked up, the high, nervous one that says something exciting has transpired in the bushes somewhere.

"A bird you've never seen! I've got a life bird for you!"

You look at your shoes. They're nice. Your slacks are nice, too. You're at work, being responsible.

"It's an upland sandpiper. Absolutely beautiful. I saw it this morning. I'll bet it's still there."

The upland part sounds good. Upland means dry, evoking visions of places devoid of standing water. One more glance at your loafers, then you nibble the bait.

"Where is this bird?"

"About 20 miles. In a hilltop meadow, with a beautiful view and lots of pastureland."

Oops. That pastureland reference throws up a red flag. You've followed the old girl to pastures before. They almost always feature soft ground where huge cow feet leave holes that fill with black water.

"Any cows around?"

"A few, I guess."

And, so, once again, it has come to this. Do you whine about shoes or plow straight for the muck? Upland sandpipers are exquisite birds. Possessed of a 20-inch wingspan, these buff-toned, foot-long shorebirds sing a winnowing song you can hear for a mile.

Formally abundant on midwestern prairies and in some eastern states, they were killed in excess by market hunters of the late 1800s. Since 1940, land use changes have adversely affected them, too. In the midwest, their prairie nesting grounds have been cultivated. In the east, much of their farmland habitat has reverted to forest. Throughout the country, grasslands have been developed for residential and industrial use.

Sighting an upland sandpiper is a momentous occasion in many parts of this bird's former range. That's what mom thinks, anyway. "You've never seen one have you?" she asks.

Pale clouds of dust swirl behind the birdmobile. Dust connotes dryness, a very good sign. But in a meadow far below—where three upland sandpipers perch on fence posts, singing songs like the sad, rising wind—beef cow tonnage has pushed hooves deep within rain-soaked soil.

"Let's park here for a moment. They just might fly up toward the road."

Let the record show you tried one last time to save your shoes.

When the birds refuse, mom pronounces the sad, awful truth. "You'll have to walk down there to see them."

In retrospect, it was no worse than usual. Deer flies attacked you. Tar pit ooze caked the cuffs on your slacks. Sweat drenched your shirt. You ripped your crotch on the first barbed wire fence.

And your loafers? The poor things succumbed in a quagmire of Hereford compost.

But you did see upland sandpipers—flying slowly overhead on stiffly beating wings; running swiftly through grassy openings on long, spindly legs; beginning each song with gurgling notes like water from a bottle, then switching, mid-call, to a loud "whip-whee-you," like the long, drawn-out cry of a hawk.

That's what you'll remember—not the torn pants and cow pies—long after good footwear has dried.

THE NEED TO SEE GREEN

He drove through the hills without saying that much, but I knew all the green had enthralled him.

Twelve hours before, he'd been home, in cental Texas, where temperatures had hovered near 100 degrees for two weeks. Leaves had been browned to a crisp around Austin. He had called on an impulse. He wanted to see green, he said.

Now he was driving through Northeastern summer, away from big cities and heat. Rain in the spring and cool weather through June had made central New York a lush garden. Hay fields were green, forest glades even greener. He had never been upstate, he said, so I drove him around.

What was he thinking, as we drove down back roads? My guess is he liked what he saw. Few places on earth are as beautiful as the Northeastern countryside in summer — especially a summer like this one.

Few have been days of oppressive humidity; few days when dogs panted and blacktop formed hot, sticky bubbles. Instead, we've had days of warm sun and dry air. Come the night, we've been sleeping with covers.

We turned down a tree-shaded road that I love, where the houses are older, the barns well-preserved and the big front-yard maples still healthy. Hay fields grew thick; roadside ditches exploded with flowers.

We drove past clumps of day lilies in orange profusion; sprays of chicory gleamed silver blue. Black-eyed Susans glowed yellow, while swarms of small insects combed Queen Anne's lace flowers for nectar.

"Things are dry down in Texas," he said as we sped through the country. Around us, green hills undulated. They rolled and they rolled, blending into each other. Every one had a forested top.

Cows abounded in pastures, their coats looking cleaner than clean. Shade from large oaks offered cool resting places where cuds could be chewed at a leisurely summertime pace.

Every turn in the road brought a bright sunny meadow, its blooms luring butterflies, beetles and bees. Was he counting the different butterflies — the hairstreaks, mourning cloaks, swallowtails, monarchs and such? Was he noting the delicate pink of the thistle blooms, the yellow of mullein, the raspberry hue of crown vetch? My guess is he was, but he didn't say much.

That night we sat out, while a cool breeze slipped down off the mountain. When high pressure surrounds us and cumulous clouds vie with brilliant blue sky all day long, we can count on this breeze come sundown.

Cool air slipped off the hillside, taking smoke from the barbecue down toward the valley below. Catbirds squawked in the honeysuckle. Saturn began peeking out from a summertime sky.

He sat in his chair, took a deep breath and said, "You should come down to Austin. It's not as pretty as this, but I still think you'll like it a lot."

I'm sure that I will, only not in the summer. In summer I'm staying right here.

"Joe," I remarked, "You should know things can get pretty sticky up here. When the wind's from the south, we get hot humid weather that sends people running for shade."

He sat in the cool summer evening and smiled. There was no way he would have believed me.

August

EVERYONE'S FAT

If I were a deer, I would freeze time this minute. I would speak to the great god of wild quadrupeds, saying, "Stop the world spinning right now."

Have you seen glossy deer, munching calmly through summer? Have you looked at the sheen on their coats and their fat, bulging sides? There are no skinny deer ribs come August in these parts— not when summer brings rain that keeps everything tropically lush.

I wake in the morning, look out and they're munching, just chewing thick grass like fat cows in a cud-chewer's heaven.

Occasionally, just for variety's sake, they will lift up their heads and chew off a wild shrub leaf or two. If berries are near—honeysuckle, blueberry and raspberry all fit the bill—they will gulp a few down for dessert.

It's been cool here this summer, and all the deer like it. Deer flies, mosquitoes and gnats haven't conquered our corner of the world. When the deer come to graze, they're not plagued by these pests. Deer ears and tails are not twitching to shake bugs away.

Bucks are still friends with each other, it seems. I watch a pair browsing with twin fawns and one silky doe. Buck antler velvet absorbs morning light and reflects it as deep rusty brown. One buck's antlers bow outward before curving back. Then they fork at the top, pushing closer together. If they grow too much longer, they'll touch.

Maybe they're last year's fawns. Maybe the doe is their mother. As one prone to schmaltz, I would like to think they're one big family.

Things certainly look harmonious out there in the mist, as the fog and the sun fight for turf. Everyone's fat; no one's thinking of rutting or fighting or finding good food. Soon apples will fall from the trees, and the field corn will ripen. If you were a deer, wouldn't this be the hour to stop time?

There aren't even people about in the woods. Occasionally someone will walk down a path, but not often in summer, when trails thicken up. Mostly, it's quiet, and the cougars are gone, so there's nothing to fear in the forest.

Spring fawns only get frightened when does say they should. But late summer fawns are stronger; they leave bigger prints in the mud than before, during May, when they wobbled a lot.

Now they run quickly when car lights appear, their sleek forms disappearing toward quieter, brushier places. Like colts, they're still frisky, but more confident. They know the woods now. They know when to be fearful.

They still have their spots, though, and they still worship mom. When she moves, they follow. When she snorts, they listen.

Time dashes past them, as it does for all creatures, but they don't let it get them depressed. Seasons whiz by; antlers come and they go. Fawn spots fade but are reborn on other deer come the next spring.

BEREFT OF PINE NEEDLES

Thumbs down on the air mattress. Ditto on foam pads that roll up for backpacking trips. Neither one offers the lumbar support human backs need when plunked on the ground.

Rotten pine needles—there's the answer. Find a large pine, place your tent underneath it and sweet dreams will follow forthwith. What give! What resilience! No more bony body parts grating against rock-hard soil. Shoulders and hips sink in softly as nature gives way.

How important is a pine needle mattress? Try sleeping on tree roots some time. Or dirt mixed with rocks. You'll wake up convinced someone's beaten you up with a pipe.

As for air mattresses, one tends to roll off them. That's because they're always popping up on the side you're not on. Roll over, and they want you to keep on rolling. Also, there's the subliminal fear something sharp will appear, and your bed will explode in the night.

Foam pads aren't much better. Many are manufactured short and thin, so they'll fit on a backpack and not be that heavy. So far so good, but when night comes, you feel rocks in your back, everything from your knees down is on the ground and you slide off that slippery cover that enwraps the foam.

There's a bright side, however. Getting a poor night's sleep outdoors beats a poor one indoors every time. When you can't sleep indoors, you just lie there second-guessing all the dumb decisions you've made in your life. Outdoors, you lie awake and wonder what creature just grunted or yowled near the tent. At least that's a learning experience.

In recent weeks—while reposing on air mattresses, foam pads and earth without sleeping—I've heard numerous creatures. Most of the time it was pitch dark when I heard them.

Occasionally, shafts of moonlight cut through deep forest growth. Almost every time, the sounds shattered dead silence. Once or twice, creatures called while a night wind prevailed, stirring leaves into incessant motion.

Several times deer came upon the campsite. Upon whiffing humans, they snorted and stamped their hooves. Other nights saw foxes screaming 25 feet away, raccoons making churring sounds climbing trees overhead and screech owls whistling wavering calls through the dark.

After all of these nights came the dawn, which is also a bright spot for outdoor insomniacs. It's been coming around 5:00 a.m. lately. If I'd been sleeping, I would have missed it, which would have been a shame, because that's when the birds are still singing.

Even now, with August upon us, cardinals, catbirds, wood pee-wees and other songbirds still call briefly when night fades away. Chickadees, bluejays and tufted titmice also flit through the woods, every one of them chirping or buzzing.

Several mornings ago, what may have been the last singing wood thrush of the year blessed the woods with a flute serenade. The concert took place at 5:23 a.m. Bereft of pine needles, I hadn't slept well and was able to catch every note.

TURTLES LIVE LONGER

Warm encounters with reptiles are not only possible, they're rewarding.

Granted, one must choose one's ectotherm friends with great care. Not every cold-blooded creature enjoys eyeballing humans up close. Snapping turtles are a lost cause, as are rattlesnakes sunning themselves. Garter snakes fall in the middle somewhere. If you give them their space, they'll permit you to watch their tongues flick.

Things warm quite a bit when we move on to red-bellied snakes. People who fear all snakes should hold one of these 8-inch creatures. No biting, no hissing, no spitting, no slime.

And then there are box turtles. Box turtles are reptiles, but there's something about them that can warm the mammalian heart.

They're small, which is nice. A big box turtle goes 6 inches long. They're pretty as well, sporting domelike shells splashed with yellow-orange blotches on an olive background.

Found throughout most of the eastern United States, box turtles also invite terrestrial encounters by living their lives on dry land. Try buddying up to a painted turtle, and you'll see why this matters. Painted turtles lie semi-submerged for what seems like half their lives. You need swim fins to reach them. When you do, they decide making friends isn't smart, so they slide from their logs and are gone.

Not so with the box turtle, a creature of open woodlands, fields and stream banks. On a hot day, a box turtle may soak in a pond or just wallow in mud for a while, but most of the time, it prefers hunting up snails, worms and berries on land. People can walk in the woods and chance upon it. When they do, scaly wonders await.

This reporter recently observed a box turtle closely. He came away enriched. The turtle appeared to gain less from the encounter. It did play along, though. What more could one ask?

Momentarily detained from its ponderous meanderings along a back-country road, the box turtle seemed only mildly miffed at being picked up, photographed and admired. Its clawed feet never flailed. Hissing and snapping did not come to pass. The turtle just looked its admirer in the eye — the encounter took place at human eye level — and waited patiently for this meeting of species to end.

Patience is a virtue in turtles. Put yourself in this situation, and compare your reaction to that of a turtle: You're walking along, munching slugs. It's a moist day, so they're out. Life is good. Oops, there's a guy. He picks you up, stares you in the face and puts you back down.

Then comes the worst part. As you waddle away, all engines full at about 100 yards per hour, the guy runs up ahead, sprawls on his belly and shoots pictures as you labor toward the privacy you so deservedly seek. When you've gone 50 yards, he picks you back up, takes you back to the place you started and suggests you do it again.

The turtle in question just kept on keepin' on. In the world of nature photography, there are close-ups and there are habitat shots. A guy can't do it all in one shooting. The turtle seemed to grasp this intuitively. No problem, my photographer friend. Just make sure to highlight my good side.

When the session concluded, I thought of two things. A box turtle has a hinge on its lower shell that can flip up and join with its upper shell in times of danger. Before the two shells meet, the turtle retracts its head behind them. The resulting seal is so tight a knife can't slip through it.

The box turtle I photographed never resorted to this. That was nice, was it not? It must have deemed me a harmless pest, albeit a persistent one.

The second thought focused on living a long time. Box turtles are among the oldest of all living vertebrates. Numerous individuals have lived more than a century. How do they do it?

It must be the mellow lifestyle. Box turtles don't get excited. They do one thing at a time, and they do it well. What's the big hurry, anyway? Relax and look around. You'll find more slugs that way.

THE LAST WINGS OF SUMMER

The wings of autumn don't wait quite that long. By the last week of August they're beating toward life farther south.

Take a stroll by the river. Walk a field with its hay stubble turning pale brown. You'll hear the wings and see them.

Some are insistent, beating south as if a blizzard were coming. Others carve circles over places the birds hate to leave.

Barn swallows insist while ospreys and gulls linger longer. They're all moving south by September, but only the swallows seem driven by forces that won't let them rest.

How quickly, how subtly, the swallows leave home. One late August morning, they natter on wires. The next, only silence remains. No sickle-shaped wings dip to capture farm pond insect life. No familiar blue shapes argue summer won't end as they dive while the sun quickly sets. They're gone now—a steady blue stream heading east toward the ocean, where they'll follow the coast in a line over dunes toward a world northern farmers don't know. Argentina beckons. Costa Rica demands equal time.

Sit on a beach and count barn swallows over the dunes. You'll feel the urgency of changing seasons. You'll wish swallows viewed change in the same way as ospreys and gulls.

The gulls are ring-bills, hatched out farther north. Now they toy with migration, swirling southward in fits. If a golf course appeals, they'll linger a fortnight, gleaning insects from fairways and rough. If the mornings are mild and bug morsels abound, they may stay until leaves turn, or snow flies, or longer. While most inland ring-bills will end up at the ocean, a few will decide that they needn't smell salt air at all. No desperate need overwhelms them. No clock ticks, reminding them time has run out.

And ospreys? They dally with purpose. When one looks up and sees them, one feels they will go, but not quickly, not without finding fish.

Perhaps their long journey began in the mountains, then meandered down rivers that lead toward the coast. Rivers with shallows and carp slow them down. The pickings come easy. Just circle and circle, then hover, then dive. Ospreys that locate good fishing move on with reluctance. They'll linger for days, their large, elbowed wings black and white against a cobalt blue sky.

Those are the best days, when late summer skies are that blue. Cool northern breezes dispel all the haze that the Gulf Coast sent up for dog days. Goldenrod yellow seems brighter than sun. Days dawn like September but warm up more like August by noon. A circling osprey folds its wings, then plummets toward prey in the water. There's a splash, a brief struggle, before victor and vanquished rise into the air.

It's a small fish, eight inches, a summer repast soon converted to strength for flights later on. Around and around flies the victor, in search of a good dining perch. No hurry, no rush, just a series of circles. No haste, no abruptness, only summer receding on tomorrow's cool northerly breeze.

September

FIRST DAY OF SCHOOL

Cue up the video, the one labeled, "First Day of School." Shot last September, it stars two summer children, a fog-enshrouded bus and leaves turning yellow from drought. The leaves tell a story, so please watch the tape.

Enter the cherubs, eating breakfast on day number one. The girl is five. Don't those pigtails look great? There's the boy, all of nine, string-bean straight, deeply tanned.

Breakfast consumed, they proceed down the driveway. Each one pokes and meanders, pretending it's summer, somehow knowing it's fall. Spider webs drip, each a circular death trap, gleaming with wet glassy jewels. Goldenrods nod while the kids pick grass switches. The cat yawns and follows along.

There's a tell-tale rumbling from just up the road; an eminence pushing through fog. The bus rolls to a stop, there's a gaseous hydrolic whooshing, a panicked kiss or two, the closing of accordian doors and sad departure, summer's end.

Round the bend rolls the bus and it's gone. Birds fuss again, insects hum. The camera pans back up the driveway, where the cat, like a sphinx, sits and waits. Above her large oaks yearn for water. Their leaves clatter dryly; a microphone captures their thirst. They've been scorched for three months now, these red oaks and maples, deprived of the moisture they need. Their leaves show the strain, yellow-brown from the heat. A canopy, threadbare, lets sunlight pour through.

That was last summer — parched, humid, exhausting. This year we saw none of that. Rain has fallen to nurture and soften. Oak branches arched over shaded driveways. Every forest walk felt woodsy, not dry.

Rivers ran high throughout most of the summer. Gardens survived without hoses and watering cans. Mushroom fanatics found boletes abundant. Chanterelles seemed to pop out on every old stump.

Beavers heard water that gurgled and had to be stopped. Herons found something to keep their knees wet. Mosquitoes emerged as a twilight armada, intent on bare ankles and spots behind knees.

Kids everywhere grew taller, learned more of life's lessons. They played through the summer like nothing but sunny days mattered.

When the bus comes tomorrow, that lush life for children will end. The girl wears her hair in braids now, not pigtails. The boy's still a string bean. It's just that the bean has stretched out. Will they look fondly back as the bus drives away and think, "Gosh, what a nice place to live?" They're too young for that now, but things change, you know. Twenty-five summers hence, when the oaks loom like giants, they will know what they had during summers both wet and bone dry.

IT SMELLS LIKE SEPTEMBER

Silence at dawn can mean only one thing: Summer's grip on our world has relaxed. Two months ago, if you slept in a tent, dawn exploded with countless bird songs. Even before dawn, wood thrushes played flutes through new leaves sagging with dew. Cardinals out-whistled each other. Tom turkeys gobbled, then strutted, then fanned.

Now, days awaken as if tranquilized. You can lie on your back in the woods and count on one hand the attempts by bird voices to sing. A cardinal starts up and then stops. There's a half-hearted song from a male yellow-throat.

Chickadees break the silence, but they chatter of autumn, not spring. A family group buzzes by, all excited. They squeak, churr and buzz, then depart. When they're gone, it turns quiet, like a woods without leaves in the cold.

Songs grow outdated as summer days ripen. August's last fledglings have leapt toward their freedom. Mates no longer need finding. Territories no longer need defending. Egg fragments line nests that deer mice soon will cover and claim.

Adults molt their feathers while August progresses. While they do, they can't fly, so they stay mum and keep out of sight. Soon insects will drone through the day and night, but these days they are still tuning up. So we wake in the woods without benefit of a natural alarm. We hear change in the silence. We think seasons are blinks of an eye.

It seems, overnight, that the roadsides turned white. Teams of gnomes came to plant Queen Anne's lace. How did every old field change its face since last week — from green to a goldenrod yellow?

Go sit in a field and look around. Goldenrod is everywhere, along with milkweed that might have been there yesterday but wasn't four feet tall and thick with blooms.

How do such things sneak up and grab us so fast? How come, overnight, the world is filled with Jerusalem artichokes, bright yellow and bold as the sun? Why wasn't there an adjustment period, a time of acceptance?

There was, but the signs were too subtle. When they weren't, we preferred not to see. Every day since the equinox, the weatherman has told us we're losing our days while the nights slowly lengthen. I hear but refuse to accept.

Yes, that is the first hint of purple on maples, but who wants to dwell on it yet? Indeed, the tree swallows did leave for Central America two weeks ago, but aren't they quite early this year?

Shorebirds pass through from the Arctic. The phone rings. . . "I've seen yellowlegs." Cats chase grasshoppers. Ten thousand tomatoes all ripen at once.

It's such a short cycle. Can't someone delay it? My only thought here is to seize it, enjoy it, be part of it while it's still here. Don't hesitate until frost tells you time has run out.

Already I burrow much deeper at night, pull my sleeping bag over my ears. Soon crickets will play violins for the moon, and the morning will sound like September.

LET'S GO BACK TO THE TREES

We came down from the trees, and just maybe it's time we went back.

I went back recently—not in an evolutionary sense, but to have a cold drink in a treehouse my friend Mike had built. Ten minutes up there, and I knew the lowdown on treehouses: They're not built for kids; they're for parents.

Mike went up first, which I thought might be best. If the darn thing collapsed, I assumed he would want to fall first. But it didn't. In fact, his arboreal roost proved as solid a house as the third little pig's brick abode. Twelve feet high, in the fork of an old apple tree, it accommodated three adults simultaneously that hot afternoon. Not once did it shimmy or creak.

Two step ladders got us up there, each one nailed to the tree in a manner that made us feel safe. While we climbed up, the old apple's trunk climbed up with us, its gray peeling bark tempting fingers to reach out and touch. What a wonderful tree, this provider of sauces and pies. Every fall, white-tailed deer gather under its branches. Every spring, honeybees comb its flowers. And now, a new era—the treehouse decade—has begun.

We opened a green door and stepped into the house. It was magic up there in that tree. Here was a room, maybe 4 feet by 6 feet, that looked down at summer's abundance. At both ends of the room, Mike had built benches. with a fold-up table in between.

Sitting on either bench, you could look out a window on every side. Three sides featured small shuttered openings, while the fourth boasted a picture window-sized view of the world.

What a view out that grand picture window. Staring through branches, ripe apples and leaves, we looked down at a goldenrod meadow. The meadow stretched up a gentle slope for 100 yards before meeting a forest that covered the top of the hill.

There were so many dimensions, so many textures, so many feelings up there.

If you wanted, you could focus on a tree branch 12 inches away. You could look for caterpillars or lose yourself in the texture of old apple bark. Four feet away, house finch males pecked at seeds from a feeder.

Up above, out of sight, several goldfinches chattered. Down below, you just knew, if you sat still and waited, deer with sleek rufous coats would arrive to eat apples at dusk.

Overhead, sunlight beat down on apple tree leaves. While a soft breeze caressed them, leaves twitched, bouncing sunbeams. Colors danced through the branches—a dappled mosaic of gray, gold and green.

Now I know kids have problems and pressures and all. And I know they need places where the weight of the world falls away. But adults are the ones who should sit in treehouses. Adults are the ones who could use a reminder that life isn't all paying bills.

Not ready to leave, Mike looked out at the meadow. "My wife and I read the paper up here," he said. "Sometimes we'll have a drink here in the evening or just bring a book up and sit."

To date, Mike reported, his kids have reacted coolly to the treehouse. They've got video games in the house, and their bikes in the driveway to ride.

But wait until they're older. Then they'll come climbing. Wait until adulthood has weighed them down, and they need to be kids once again.

SAW DUST ADDICTION

On a recent Sunday afternoon, I saw four people walking in the forest. It was a beautiful day—gorgeous leaves, azure sky—and I watched to see what they were up to.

They were up to a walk, pure and simple—no great master plan. Their pace lacked a cadence; they ebbed and they flowed, rolling easily like fog through the woods.

I hid behind a tree and pondered this. Just walking. No other reason to be there. No chain saw. No splitter. No donkey cart filled with cut wood needing someone to push it.

Somehow, these people had scurried away when the wood-cutting trap had been sprung. Somehow, they had managed to stave off addiction to autumnal saw dust and trees getting split into chunks.

I envied those folks with their light summer clothing. Chitty chat, watch the birds, soak in autumn's great show. Just enjoy the outdoors. At all costs, avoid sweat and swear words and the torture of wood.

Chunks of the stuff lay in scattered profusion around me: termite food, cellulose, black birch I'd cut months ago and had left on the ground. Next to the pile sat the donkey cart, needing its donkey.

Spare me, oh great woodland spirit who dwells in this forest. Cast a deep spell, turn me into a frog—just as long as I no longer want to cut wood when I wake. Fill me with loathing for two-cycle oil and the snarl of the engine it feeds. Make me a stroller, a chatter, a looker—an unburdened member of autumn's great leaf-peeping chorus.

The walkers strolled off up a hill toward a meadow. Sun-dappled ash leaves fell slowly toward earth. A breeze from the north seemed to nudge them but not push too hard.

I looked at a chunk of black birch, and my hands started sweating. I needed to pick it up, needed to sniff it. I needed to split it in two. A stack of it started to build in my mind, piling high, drying out in the wind.

One last time I entreated the spirit to free me—from wood mauls and wedges and dropping large things on my toes. If so freed, I agreed, I would kiss the oil man when he came.

Nothing happened. A crow cawed. I knew I was still the same slave. Goodbye, lucky strollers. Yours truly, the donkey, must start loading birch in his cart.

It smelled good, that birch did, even after six months on the ground. Remember how good it smelled right when it fell? All that wintergreen essence? Every snapped twig exuded the scent.

Remember how good it felt, all through last winter, when birch turned to coals and chilled toes wriggled happy and warm?

Remember the thousands of times, cutting wood, when a wildlife encounter transpired? Or the thousands of times, at the end of the day, when two friends stopped their chopping or turned off their saws, and watched purple streaks stain the horizon?

A donkey's life really is not so enslaving. It speaks to an outlook on life that says simple is good.

The cart slowly filled. I smelled many a chunk. Then I pushed and I grunted and brayed like an ass. Another wood season had started.

October

HANDS ON A SEASONAL CLOCK

It's a sneaky sensation, the coming of fall. Nothing happens overtly. No changes occur so abruptly that heads snap around. Instead, fall arrives like a cloaked interloper, an eavesdropper hiding behind every tree we walk by. If we turn around quickly, the cloaked figure fades like thin fog when it's hit by the sun.

Change? Around here? But the leaves look the same—not much redder than minutes ago. The air feels the same—not much colder, or damper, than when we set out through the woods.

Yet, this month that will steal summer from us is changing our world. October works slowly, its days overlapping. Changes creep forward like hands on a seasonal clock.

Day to day, hour to hour, we hardly take notice.

Are the maples more crimson today than they were yesterday? They are, but our eyes can't perceive such a slight alteration. We don't register the subtle ascendance of reds over greens. We can't measure slow death in a chlorophyll cell or the gradual exodus birds undertake in the fall.

Time-lapse photogrpahy — that's what we need. Time-lapse photographers condense natural events that take weeks into ones that take minutes. They do this by filming a single location at regular intervals over a given period. When they play the film back, they speed everything up, so clouds race through the sky and the petals on flowers unfurl with incredible speed.

If we had such a film about fall, we would watch open-mouthed. Imagine October condensed into five or 10 minutes. In the blink of an eye, leaves would turn red and fall. Mountains of sweet corn would swell in farm markets, then shrink just as fast as they grew.

An acorn would tumble, then a dozen, then hundreds. A torrent of acorns would hammer the ground, with squirrels attacking them, blue jays jabbing them like jackhammers, deer chewing their nut-meats non-stop.

White-tailed deer coats would go through their change while we watched, from a thin rusty red to a thick gray highlighted with brown. Antlers would lose fuzz in seconds, then harden. Their points would grow sharp, gleaming white like smooth ivory tusks.

Apples would tumble, and days would grow shorter. Tomatoes would leap into jars. Crickets would sing, then shut up and then die. Fog would continue to thicken.

In an instant green grass would turn brown; frost would come. Firewood piles would sprout up beside sheds. While smoke flowed from chimneys, a stream of raptors would soar by, racing south on the wind toward tomorrow.

Below in the bushes, a bustle of songbirds — their frenzied attacks on the ripe fruits of dogwoods would strip the shrubs bare in a minute. We might count tens of thousands of birds that brief moment, then see none in the next as they left us for points farther south.

Hold the phone, stop the movie; it's going too fast. No one wants to see nature like this. Days in October are meant to be savored. Changes are meant to seep in and envelope us slowly. Continuity counts for a lot in the natural world.

These days, when I wake up, I lie there and watch the red leaves on a big maple tree. Slowly the red army conquers the green. This morning, I think I saw new red recruits, but the truth is, I can't quite be sure.

LOVE ON A GREAT DAY FOR GEESE

Michael got hitched on a great day for geese — chilly wind from the north; lots of ominous clouds; people wishing they lived farther south.

I doubt he approved of the sky when he woke. People who marry in October outdoors like to think the big day will highlight their love and the brilliance of autumn's bright palette. They sit on their decks in July and imagine: all those colors aflame, golden aspens, red maples in scarlet. Corn stalks will rustle. Warm sun will beat down. Apples will glisten as if they'd been buffed by a cloth.

That's the way young people, madly in love, seem to think in July: optimistic. But what are the odds this bright day will appear as predicted? It didn't, of course. Michael and Chris's day grouched and then glowered, from dark gloomy start to the end.

However, the indomitable spirit of humankind prevailed. Vows of love were exchanged, which made all in attendance feel warmed by communal good feelings. The bride fairly dazzled—white dress on tan shoulders; eyes sparkling clear, as cool blue as a glacier's meltwater. As for the groom, not renowned as a dazzler, he stepped out in his nuptial plumage—a tux—which, on someone whose normal attire is old sneakers, made everyone feel like a party.

Here's more good news: Not one raindrop fell on the head of a guest or killed the fizz in a full champagne glass. This wedding watcher would like to think he stopped the rain by intense brainwave action.

Shortly after dawn he awoke to see clouds and hear telltale autumnal goose honkings. Geese in the sky? That means a west wind or a north one. If Chris wears a short dress, or one without shoulders, she'll freeze standing out on that deck.

So the goose watcher started to chant incantations. Driving out to the woods where big chunks of red maple lay waiting for someone to split them, he invoked the spirit of the great Canadian honker. Michael's cold day was a honker's bonanza. Wedge after wedge of geese sailed past the treetops as mauls clobbered wedges and migration hurried along.

The goose watcher chanted in time with his chopping: Let there be geese flying over the wedding. Let the preacher pause briefly, let solemnity reign, and then let heavy honking commence. Let all in attendance look up to see chevrons, a squadron of geese, looking down, honking loudly, like Blue Angels tipping their wings in a passing salute.

And, Great Goose, one more thing: Please don't let it rain. You can have your north wind; we all know you require it. Just don't let the clouds open up.

The goose watcher split wood for three hours that morning. He spoke to the geese all the while. Then he dashed home, unloaded his cache of red maple, quickly tied on a noose (a necktie) and took off for the wedding.

They stood on the deck and the pastor said things about sharing. The skies held their ground, grey as concrete, but not spitting rain. But where were the geese? The right time came and sadly it went.

"Til death do you part?" asked the preacher and poor Michael gulped. Time stopped for a moment. Cue the geese! Sound the trumpets! Let honking prevail! Let the couple receive nature's blessing!

They didn't show up, not a single lost goose. Michael said that he did, that he would for all time, and great smooching ensued in the cold. Within moments, a band of party animals leapt forth, and the goose watcher strained to be with them.

People went to a tent. Food and champagne appeared. Soon all thinking of rain and of geese were forgotten as disc jockies spun favored platters. Once, while the DJ cued up Mustang Sally, the goose watcher heard distant voices. Outside, very high, through the darkness they flew, wishing Michael and Chris love forever.

WOOLLY BEAR KILLERS

If you'll permit an editorial comment, the world needs a few fewer highway billboards and a few more woolly bear caterpillar preserves.

I have nothing against billboards per se. The fact is, you wouldn't know where the nearest frontier town or water slide was if a sign didn't rear up from the woods to inform you.

Where I draw the line is at woolly bear murder. It burns me up when Americans drive blithely along, reading billboards, while their tires are squashing these fine creatures.

I know it's happening. Over the past several weeks—during the height of woolly bear season—I've driven with several people whose eyes have not stayed on the road.

Woolly bear killers! That's what they were, while they drove along vacuously, telling me autumn was pretty. Couldn't they see all those woolly bear bodies? They could have, if only they'd looked.

By simply watching the road, I have seen—and avoided—hundreds of woolly bears inching their way across highways. I simply adjusted the steering wheel ever so slightly upon seeing one, approached on that set angle and—voila!—a woolly bear was saved.

Before we continue, please don't tell me I have a trained eye, and therefore I see these things when others don't. It doesn't matter. The responsibility for saving woolly bears rests with the motorist.

Let's not forget that humans are the stewards of this planet. We have the brain power. We are the visionaries. Your average woolly bear is dumb as a stick. When it turns into a moth, it will knock itself silly trying to mate with a porch light.

Only we motorists can save them. They can't do it by themselves. To do this we must first identify, then appreciate, then avoid.

Identification is easy. Black at both ends and brown in the middle, woolly bear caterpillars are about 1 1/2 inches long and covered with short, stiff hairs. Some people think you can tell how cold the winter will be by gauging the relative width of the brown middle band as compared with the black terminal bands, but you can't.

Woolly bears also are easy to appreciate. One appreciates through knowing, so here's some life history. After overwintering as caterpillars under logs or bark, they awaken in spring, eat a few green plants and then pupate in a cocoon they have made from their own body hairs.

The moth that emerges will be buff-colored and nondescript, with a wingspan of about 2 inches. People will call it an Isabella moth.

Right now, woolly bears are on the road so much because finding a good log under which to burrow for winter requires extensive travel.

For the fullest appreciation of a woolly bear, pick one up. When you do, it will curl in a ball for protection., Harmless, it will roll in your hand like the smoothest of marbles. You'll find it one of the softest, gentlest creatures in nature, totally at your mercy. Drop it softly in the grass. Let it go on its way.

After you do this, you'll cherish woolly bears and want to preserve them. How can you do this? For starters, stop running them over. Every time you avoid one, imagine Mr. Nature is gumming a big silver star on your forehead.

Besides woolly bear avoidance, I propose the installation of woolly bear crossing signs on roads that experience heavy caterpillar use.

Would you slow down for a woolly bear? Dig deep, and respond from the soul.

THE SOFT SIDE OF LIFE

A swamp exists; therefore, it is.

Muddy and methane-filled — cold in October — it beckons to those who accept it without false illusions.

One goes to a swamp to feel mud on the bottom. Slick as grease in some sections, like quicksand in others, it serves as a barrier, keeping the fainthearted out.

One goes to a swamp to hear primeval noises and wonder what made them; what beast with wet skin, bulging eyes and a yen for pond scum.

A male, tired of being a wimp, can walk through a swamp to feel manly. There's no doubt it's macho sashaying through duckweed at dusk while the herons are croaking.

This swampoholic has, for years, reaffirmed his manhood by facing the ooze and surviving. For years he has visited swamps feeling Spartan, eschewing the comforts that lazy men need to survive. Give him the swamp and a thin pad to sleep on. Let him exhaust himself. Let him eat beans from a can.

And then came the hot tub—insidious tempter—and Iron Man felt himself slipping.

Please understand. Iron Man himself never would have suggested the option of renting a place with a tub.

"Let us sleep in a tent," he had said to his friend when they talked of their upcoming swamp visit. His friend had agreed. That's what macho men do. They drive hundreds of miles, thrash around in the mud and then sleep in a tent, cold and clammy.

And that is exactly what Iron Man and his friend would have done had not one of the two gone all squishy.

"I found this ad in a magazine—a nice place for rent. And it's right near the swamp where we're going." He of Great Softness had called Iron Man on the phone just a day before leaving. "Oh, and yes, there's a hot tub. It sits on a deck by the lake."

Iron Man had always loved that lake. He imagined that loons would be on it at this time of year. But a tub? Pure indulgence, a shameless admission the user was pleasure-enslaved.

Those loons would be nice, though. And the tub was wood-fired, so a real man could split logs for hours to stifle his guilt.

Also, the place was a three-minute drive from the swamp. Let's remember the swamp, the whole reason this trip was occurring.

So it was that the Iron Man loosened his grip. They would try it just once, this plush pad on the lake, just as long as The Soft One agreed not to whisper a word. Iron Man hadn't spent all those years in the mud to let one little slip wreck his image.

The lake, ah, the lake. At 7 o'clock on a crystal-clear morning—with frost on the deck and a shroud of light mist on the water—a loon yodeled once in a wild, haunting tribute to fall.

Up to his neck in 100-degree water, Iron Man gazed through the mist and could see the loon's profile. The sun had just risen. It crept above pines on the opposite shore, casting warm, golden light on the steam that arose from the tub.

Our hero then raised his left arm from the depths. It steamed like the mist on the lake. He held out his hand, and a coffee mug filled it. His friend had just brewed up a pot and would join him to wallow.

Wedges of geese wavered over that morning. Kinglets played games in the hemlocks. Maples glowed magically, yellow and orange. Not one human sound touched the lake.

They turned on the jets, then they steamed like two lobsters— The Soft One and his newly-found clone. They would get to the swamp around noon, they decided.

Sure, all the action of dawn would have passed. But real men, they agreed, need much more than swamp slogging. They have soft sides, as well, that need soothing to make them feel whole.

November

SOUNDS IN THE SILENCE

What does it say about life in these times that true silence can bring us up short? It says we need hums, nagging whines and some whirring. We need motors to keep us alive.

When they all take a break and true silence returns, it seems eerie, somehow out of place. Noise of some sort is the norm in our lives. When power lines fail, we camp out in the silence, afraid. When we walk outdoors, cock an ear and hear nothing, we think maybe the world's at an end.

Some of us do, but not all. Even now, in the Age of Loudness, there are those who seek silence to think. It's not easy, they'll tell you, especially near a city, where the drone of car armies rides hither and yon on the wind.

It's equally hard in one's own neighborhood, where shovels scrape sidewalks and snowblowers roar. Even country folks find silence can be elusive. Dairy farm pumps chug-a-lug through the darkness. A trail bike resounds for what seems like 10 miles.

There are ways to find quiet, however. Some require staying up past the late news, when the rest of the world has gone to sleep. Others demand being up and about on days when others stay put in their beds.

It's easy to find those who seek silence at night. Your headlights disturb them on both sides of midnight: the dog walkers, joggers and owl-watching strollers who sort things out under moonlight.

As for those who seek quiet while sunlight abounds, they like Sundays and holidays best.

Sundays find church goers getting up early, but they're thoughtful folks, mostly, not prone to disturbing the peace. Holidays dawn even more quietly. People get up late and remain in their houses. Car traffic is down. Truckers still shift through the gears, but they're dreaming. It takes place at home in the sack.

A friend called to say he'd gone out at 8:30 a.m. Thanksgiving Day. The outside world reveled in calm, so he said. I believed him. Here's what he could hear:

He heard nothing for starters—no cars tires, no shouts, no jet planes. Not a breath of wind stirred. Chimney smoke rose in a column of white. Bluejays swooped down from the treetops toward feeders. He watched without moving, he said. They lowered their wing flaps like airplanes. The jays braked and dropped by degrees. None of this made the slightest sound. They came and they went silently.

There was snow on the ground, so my friend simply stood there. No crunching of boots on dry powder ensued, only sounds his footsteps would have killed. He heard woodpecker claws as they scratched up a tree. He heard caws from a crow echo off a far hillside, then fade for what seemed like forever.

A nuthatch pair chatted; my friend claims he heard both the male and the female, and their voices had different tones. Juncos played tag through a tangle of rose hips. My friend, whom I trust, claims he heard when their wings hit a branch.

Then he swore he heard this, which I can't quite believe. A breath of wind blew, and it fluttered the leaves on an oak tree. The leaves didn't flutter, really; they just twirled very slowly, rotating on stems that would soon let them drop to the ground. My friend said the leaves never rubbed on each other, but he still heard them sway in the wind.

That's how quiet the world was that day in the snow. Be advised; Christmas morning is next.

ORION WAS SLIGHTLY ASKEW

Jack Frost must be in therapy. How else could he handle the cruel cards November has dealt him?

Yours truly prides himself on being well-balanced, and even he is having a hard time with November this year. Imagine poor Jack. One minute he's welcomed, the next he's been banished. As harbingers of winter go, this guy doesn't know which way is up.

Maybe it's the greenhouse effect. Maybe Innuits near the Arctic Circle are burning more walrus blubber for home heating fuel, and the fumes have upset the jet stream.

Whatever the reason, November is not what it once was. It used to be November got cold—and stayed there. Now November gets cold in between spates of blazing sun and monsoon-like downpours.

One day last week, I sunbathed. I saw Holsteins doing it, too. Clean-looking cows basked in green, sunny pastures, their bellies on ground still exuding a summer-like warmth.

I'm not saying we should get out our Bibles and begin pondering past sins against nature, but the situation is disquieting. One recent day I took a drive and a walk through November's quixotic environs. By sunset I felt schizophrenic.

Three days earlier, all the world had seemed frozen. Bitter wind had slammed into the Northeast from somewhere northwest of Chicago. Through the night, through the morning, it beat on the house, finding corners to moan in while wind chimes made chaotic sounds.

Snow fell and built up. Skim ice formed on the river. People scurried around cutting wood. "Wow, this is winter," I heard one man say. It was almost as if he enjoyed it.

That was three days ago, with squalls turning skies over western horizons jet black. On the day of my trip, things had changed. Temperatures would hit the low 70s by afternoon. A soft breeze caressed lazy folds of American flags. If one walked through this day and chose which way to look, one could focus on all the four seasons.

In an overgrown field, I found pockets of snow. They were tucked against hummocks that kept the sun off them all day. The rest of the field featured brown grasses blending with green.

November's normal patina in fields is the color of wheat straw—or cedar shakes weathered by decades of coastal salt wind. This year the greens are competing with tans. I sat in the grass, turned my face to the sun, and it beat on me warm like the summer.

Out on the lake, ring-billed gulls bobbed pure white. Hen mallards quacked as if winter were pure foolishness. A heron flapped by on implacable wings. If things stay like this—and no ice forms on marsh and stream edges, it can find food all winter right here.

The same can be said for the red-tailed hawk legions I saw from sunrise to sunset. If no winter snows cover farm fields, they can find all the voles they require. If the snows come and voles hide beneath them, the hawks will fly south, searching out snowless fields and their bounty.

A week ago rough-legged hawks swirled above these same fields. They had just filtered down from the tundra, as they do every year, to spend winter here, feeding on mice.

A week before that heavy rains had poured down. My river had turned Mekong-brown from a gun-metal blue.

I don't know what it means, folks. While I sunbathed, I tried not to think. That night, when I looked up, Orion was right where it should be. Tilted sideways in a low eastern sky, the hunter seemed slightly askew, like this month of November.

SQUIRRELS AREN'T SCHOLARS

The ground is in the news again. Things have been falling on it — leaves, for example — so people are looking down more than usual. Squirrels, wind and gravity are the cause.

Throw in the sun for good measure. If the Northern Hemisphere didn't start turning away from it at this time of year, trees wouldn't start closing down their in-house food factories and laying off leaves.

If the wind didn't blow, those leaves would hang tough until hard frost convinced them to fall. As for gravity, everyone knows it's around — a grand presence, but subtle.

If you don't put a belt on, your pants will droop; if you don't stay in shape, the northern part of your body will migrate toward the southern part.

But sometimes gravity speaks rather loudly. Once I slept in a house over which red oak trees towered. I lay in bed and heard acorns striking a tin roof like marbles, then rumbling down toward the gutter. That's gravity; hungry squirrels often use it to make sure they have plenty to eat.

These days, all sorts of territorial disputes are being mediated in the treetops where most squirrels live. Tempers flare as normally mild-mannered rodents start kicking each other out of oak trees they've shared for six months.

Most of the problems are food-related, with red, gray and fox squirrels vying for winter feeding territories. When a victor has been proclaimed in a particular tree, that squirrel often begins severing oak twigs and watching them fall to the ground.

Attached to these leaves and branchlets are acorns in clumps. Once they've fallen, the squirrels run down, pick them up and start thinking about where to stash them.

Some of the acorns get stashed in knotholes. Others end up in the ground, buried for retrieval at a later date.

Researchers, who have snooped on squirrels much longer than I could without going crazy, say some of these buried nuts never get found. The squirrels forget where they put them.

On the other hand, squirrels find a good many nuts, so they don't starve to death over winter. The nuts they don't find germinate in the spring and grow up to provide acorn bounty. As far as the big picture goes, this arrangement is second to none.

It's tough on the squirrels — all that burying and forgetting. Were humans to try it, the stress would lay most of us low.

Have you ever watched a squirrel bury a nut? As experiences go, it is surprisingly deep. Will there be another spring? Is there never respite from toil on life's treadmill? Squirrels provide grist for a thinker's mind mill.

I was grinding away on these thoughts just last week. Great chattering had drawn me into a woodland resplendent with white, red and chestnut oaks.

Because squirrels aren't scholars, you can get very close if you're smart. Two gray squirrels were arguing high in an oak, so whenever their squabble attained an especially fevered pitch, I took a few steps forward.

Shortly, I found myself directly below them. Glued to the trunk, they crouched 10 feet apart, staring daggers. From the larger one's mouth bulged an acorn.

First came a face-off, as both squirrels growled and jerked their tails like wildly twitching snakes. Then a chase ensued, with the nut-bearing squirrel dominating. When its rival had scampered through oak limbs toward trees in the distance, the victor descended, the acorn still stuck in its mouth.

Great digging followed, right under the tree. A burial process began. Was I watching the planting of one more oak tree or the stashing of food for the winter? "Does it matter?" I wondered. Either way, nature wins in the end.

THE STATE OF THE SWAMP

It's time once again for the annual State of the Swamp address.

I offer this update on the state of muck for those of you whose active lives have precluded slogging through cattails within the past year. You've wanted to go—heaven knows, once you've had your boots sucked off, a love of the swamp gets engrained. But other commitments somehow seemed more pressing.

Well, take heart. There's still a swamp out there with your name written on it in algal slime. I've been to that swamp recently and offer the following observations as to its flora and fauna and their overall well-being:

Let's start with ducks, which are good for the soul if you watch them. They're still in your swamp, like moths rising up from black water when dawn is just a promise. Just before it gets light, hen mallards among them commence quacking in a loud, disjointed chorus. Maybe this is some sort of wake-up call, because shortly thereafter the moth squadrons start lifting off. Their silhouettes flutter against a smudged skyline that sunlight has started to pinken.

Wood ducks are the small ones, their wingbeats much faster than mallards. When they fly from the swamp, they seem driven to reach daytime feeding areas in as direct a line as possible. From Point A to Point B, they buzz like attack planes, their speed so impressive the wind sometimes screams through their wings.

Mallards and black ducks don't hurry so much. Plumper than wood ducks, they circle and circle, deciding which swamp has the richest supply of starch-laden tubers and shoots lying just under water.

If they land in the swamp, they will share space with herons—great blue ones with necks like warmed garden hoses. Recently, in your swamp, it was falling dusk and a 30-mph wind from the south had kicked up. Grass tussocks bent as the air whistled through them. Wind gusts gave birth to patterns of wildly dancing ripples, which raced here and there aimlessly.

A heron appeared 30 feet overhead, coursing downwind without a wingbeat. Then it turned suddenly, dropped its legs and descended, its wings tipping wildly to counter the force of the wind. If you've watched great blue herons, you know how difficult it should be for them to maintain aerodynamic integrity in the face of a 30-mph wind. After all, they have appendages jutting out all over the place. Their legs dangle down, that neck stretches out and those wings catch the wind like great sails.

None of this mattered that soft windy day at sundown. The heron made landing look easy. Once touchdown took place, it stood there a moment, composing itself as its grayish toes sank in the mud.

It was growing dark in the swamp. Other herons flew over, their coarse croakings signaling night's fast encroachment on day.

Snipes began making nasal squeaks reminiscent of frogs when they nearly get stepped on. Ducks started pouring back into the swamp. Flocks of geese wavered over; their plaintive honks spoke to the soul.

I sat on a muskrat house, watching the deep ruddy sky. Soon beaver noses would wedge through the water. Soon owl hoots would float on a ceaseless south wind, striking terror in swamp rabbit hearts.

Ladies and gentlemen, I'm pleased to report that the state of your swamp is inspiring. I realized this when the moon came out full and a beaver tail slapped in the dark.

But other swamps? Friends, they are still disappearing. Let's go out and save them, so more ducks can hatch and more people can watch them at dusk.

December

GIVE GRAY DAYS A CHANCE

Late autumn days in the outdoors are boring. They're sterile. No life stirs the trees.

File that pronouncement under prevailing wisdom, a body of half-truths formulated by folks who look out their bay windows and figure a walk's not worthwhile.

Granted, there are bleak days. Skies glower, limbs clatter, trees cry out for birds. Every living thing seems to have fled or dug into the ground. But for every glum day there's a good one. For each walk forsaken, there's one that you should have been on.

On a day in December, can you see everything I'm about to describe? You may have already. If not, it awaits, but there are some restrictions. For starters go out very early. Stay until sunset and stand a lot more than you walk.

As for companions, they're banned unless quiet prevails. You can whisper and nod when you feel you must share what you've seen.

Only places where you can hear what's going on are acceptable — places where people won't crash in and scare everything.

Start out by a stream and dissect all its gurgles. It will get you in sync with a quieter world and liven your senses as well. Against ice, against grass, over rocks, around islands — every gurgle is different. Streams through wet meadows attract me the most. Their waters flow smooth and unhurried. Tall grasses beside them have dried to the color of straw.

There's a down side, of course. Gurgles drown out subtle calls from above. Step back until stream sounds are muffled suggestions. Goldfinches calling will snap your head up. They dip when they fly, not like siskins which don't dip so much.

Brown creepers and kinglets might make other sounds. Both these birds whisper, but golden-crowned kinglets break theirs up in threes. If you hear just a "tseee," that's a creeper, so look at tree trunks. These tiny brown birds spiral up them in search of insect eggs and larvae. "Tsee-tsee-tsee" denotes kinglet bands roving through hemlocks. They hang upside down, combing branches for similar fare.

If you talk at this point, a red squirrel will scold you. If you don't, it might sneak from the hemlocks for food. Most of the time it stays deep in their midst, ripping small cones apart for the seeds. But for you, quiet one, the squirrel slips toward the stream bank, nips a fern leaf (still green) and retreats.

Hawks would eat the squirrel for sure if it stayed out too long. On your late autumn day, you could see a goshawk catch a squirrel. You could watch it chase grouse with the fire of death in its eyes.

If you sat for a while, it might float from the hemlocks, a gray ghost on firmly set wings. It might perch on a stub by the unhurried stream and stare down at the dry grass, intent. The goshawk's red eyes are as sharp as its talons. Pity the field mouse fate forces to make a wrong move.

A dusting of snow on a log reveals grouse tracks. They stretch in a line, heading west. On hillsides yellow apples still hang from the trees, tempting deer to stop by every day.

Would you like to see deer—really see them—one late autumn day? Deer tracks plunge in mud, leaving deep indentations. On a mat of dry grass, frozen hard so it crinkles, they leave marks that are harder to see. If you stayed out one day in late fall and looked hard, you would see deer tails waving madly, deer nostrils snorting, deer slinking through edges; deer ears pointing forward and deer eyes so brown they seemed black.

You wouldn't think this time of year was so boring if you did that. It isn't; just give it a chance.

SO MUCH FOR WINTER

Water, water everywhere, but ice should take its place.

The month, after all, is December, a time when the tilt of earth's axis should force cold through cracks in our clothing.

It's not happening, though. Late autumn, so far, has seen drizzle much more than deep snow. For every cold day, we've had two on the warm side. For every night coals glowed hot until dawn, there were two when they died for lack of attention.

On farm ponds, at midnight, a sheer icy film crystalizes. By noon the next day, not a sign of its presence remains. Likewise on the river, where kingfishers plummet toward backwater puddles that should be rock-solid by now.

Herons, rejoice. Spread the word to all fish-eating ducks that the good life is here. As long as there is warmth, minnow forms can be speared in the shallows. Forget about thoughts of migration—it looks like you'll be here all year.

It wasn't always thus. In 1976, ponds in the Northeast were frozen by early November. They stayed that way right through the winter. Some of us remember because of a boat someone left in the water too long.

It was green, that muskrat boat. It was deep forest green, with two oars. Possessed of a flat bottom and a square, angled bow, the 10-foot-long boat had been used by an old muskrat trapper until we got our hands on it. Our turn came after the fellow had died and his boxy old boat had been pulled up on shore, there to languish while nature reclaimed it.

We could have the boat, one of his relatives told us. Just come get it, and take it away.

The old trapper's lake was a few miles from ours. In a flash we had made the big switch.

The boat leaked a while when it went in the water. The time was the third week of August. No one minded, however; the little green boat seemed to fit in so well with our lives. Our lake was small, unassuming, blue collar—like our boat was. It was a match made in heaven.

Our favored style of transport was slowly, with oars making swirls one could barely perceive. That's just how the boat seemed to think we should go—slipping through spatterdock, watching bullfrogs take their ease.

That warm summer, we caught bullheads at night from the boat. We caught lots of small perch that we filleted and had with our eggs. Blackburnian warblers nested in lakeside hemlocks. Wood ducks and muskrats cut paths through thick swatches of duckweed.

Autumn brought Canada geese to the lake, where they stayed for three weeks before October winds pushed them south. After they left, we stopped fishing for perch and began catching bass, hefty large-mouths quite close to the bank. Voraciously hungry, they slammed surface lures for two weeks and then stopped overnight.

The days still were mild, though. The trees took their time turning red. Slowly, reluctantly, cottagers pulled up their boats, locked their cabins up tight and departed for civilized grounds.

We lingered. We liked watching wind through bare branches and how it stirred waves on the surface. We liked going out in the morning and kicking up ducks off the lake. Ice-up would come, but not now, not in early November.

One morning we woke, and the wind howled most fiercely. Tied next to the dock, frozen solid in place, our green boat told us winter had come.

BEING PART OF THE LAND

Familiarity may breed contempt among humans, but not where the land is concerned. When it comes to the land, one must walk it to know it. For every path walked on—and walked on again—a contour begins making sense. For every new trail beaten through alder thickets, more fragments start looking like pieces of puzzles you know.

You won't know too much the first time you go out. It's a big sprawling parcel you've befriended. It wants to confuse you, with deep-cut ravines and two streams cutting down through their shadows. On steep ravine sides, something very strange happens. Trails seem to go straight but are actually turning in circles.

The streams also curve—blue-black snakes sliding through spongy meadows. Deer hide there when threatened, bleached grass waving over their heads. As the land rises slightly, the meadows ease into a swampy woodlot filled with beaver stumps, briars and hummocks. Still higher, on slopes that drain into these lowlands, hemlock stands blot the sunlight, their low branches poking and jabbing. They block out the sky so you can't navigate by the sun.

It is beautiful land, but not easy, not simple. It demands that you put in your time before secrets unfold. If you walk for a while, sometimes taking the hard way, slopes will slowly become second nature.

You will start knowing landmarks and giving them names, like the redberry swamp, the broken tree and the chestnut rail fence. You'll know where the old fieldstone wall hasn't crumbled and where a foundation says lives were here long before you.

Then it will happen, one pre-dawn when moonlight and owl hoots are all that befriend you. It will dawn on you that no one knows this place as well as you. In the moonlight, you'll walk through the woods and not turn on your flashlight.

That's when the next phase will start kicking in. You will move from course reckonings toward thorough and subtle awareness. Because you've been out there, you'll know where the grouse sleep and where they roost in the morning to soak up the first morning sun. When the stream boils with runoff and people can't cross, you will know where an old beaver dam makes a suitable bridge.

The broken tree crossing has deer running by it. A goshawk will sit on the tree's splintered trunk, knowing squirrels sometimes happen by. Up on the hill, where the woods meets a meadow, an old dying beech tree holds carpenter ants. If you sit down and watch that beech tree, you will see pileated woodpeckers swoop in through the woods, land upon it and tear it to shreds.

Down below, by the stream, there's a giant white pine where red squirrels appear at twilight. Sit still, and they will practically run down your leg, using branch after branch as their highway.

And then there's the best place to watch the sunrise: by a forked hemlock beavers chewed up while they sharpened their teeth. Your back to the trunk, you'll be facing due east, with a half-moon above you and black sky about to turn blue.

Grouse drum there, too, even into December. Grosbeaks fly over at dawn on their first feeding runs.

Who else knows all this about your special place? No one, because it takes time to gain knowledge. It takes walking and watching
and feeling a part of the land.

STAY OUT OF THE KITCHEN

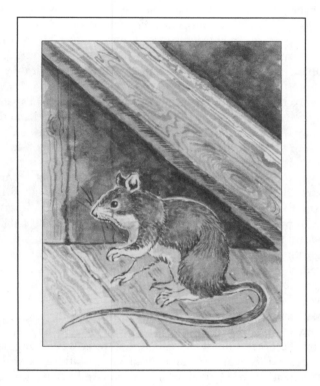

Things that go bump in the night often fill me with wonder. Skittering things prompt a feeling of wonder as well.

Skittering surged to the forefront one night recently. It was the eve of the solstice—what some people view as the essence of darkness, the nadir of all human spirit.

Unaware of the chills that would soon overwhelm me, I had driven home after work, read the paper, trimmed a tree, stoked a fire and imposed an aura of disciplinary doom on the antics of children possessed by the vacation giggles.

Outside, a soft wind from the southeast brought rain, tossing raindrops through fog that soaked red maple branches. Inside, I tossed some dry maple on coals and decided to visit Botswana's Okavango Delta via *National Geographic* magazine.

On the previous night I'd beamed myself over to Australia's northwestern coast on the wings of the same periodical. The Geographic is great on such long winter nights. Maps draw you in; color photos transport you. The world is your oyster for $21 a year.

So I gave myself up to the great Okavango. I read and I read, as I do every eve of the solstice. Children appeared by my side, and they kissed me. Timeless and dreamlike, they floated away and their voices were swallowed by sleep. I read and I read; my sweet wife said good night. Soon the clock ticked, and silence was king.

Only on the eve of the solstice can one read for what seems like 100 hours, then discover it's still very early. I looked at my watch— 10:00 p.m. Could it be?

How do people stay up late in winter? They shouldn't, I thought. Like bears, they should heed their internal flywheels, which are slowing with nature's retrenchment.

I heeded the call, hauling middle-aged bones toward a cave under grandma's fat quilt. There, as the clock said 10:30 p.m., the netherworld seeped in and turned everything charcoal gray.

It was then that they came, sometime deep in the night, happy squadrons of rodent foot racers. They had invaded an attic crawl space, on the other side of the ceiling I stare at while lying in bed. A scout danced through first, and, although its skitterings were subdued, this light sleeper bolted awake to prepare for the surge of the tide.

Something told me they had come, with their Winter Olympics— legions of rodents, each one with a gold medal dream. The sprints started first; 15 feet was the distance.

Man, they could fly. Tiny feet whirred like mad, dashing over the flat ceiling panels. The first heat seemed focused on white-footed mice, or so it appeared by the fine clacking sound of their claws.

Time was when I'd hear mice above me and not sleep for hours. Time was when I'd think about murder and mousedom's demise. A man has to mellow, however. He can't hone that sharp edge forever. I lay there and thought of their eyes, huge and soft, gleaming wet like the raindrops that fell. I thought of how cute they look, staring out at me from birds' nests they usurp in winter.

I lay in my bed on the eve of the solstice and gave Mouse Olympics my blessing. Two cats still will hunt in the house every night. If invasions dictate, traps will wait on the shelves of the pantry. But maybe there's room for a guy and his mice.

Stay out of the food, and this man will stay mellow. Stay out of the kitchen, my friends, and the attic is yours.

PART TWO
OTHER PLACES

NORTH COUNTRY SUMMER

Being a black bear entails certain discomforts.

Junk food from tourists can upset the stomach, and thick brush makes walking a chore. There are hunters in fall who would make you a rug and park rangers who dart you with drugs if you wear out your welcome.

No, a bear's life is fine if you're born into same, but I wouldn't be one in my next incarnation—unless the blueberry crop had been good and New York's Adirondack Mountains served up ample portions.

Then I would revel in being a bear, lumbering hither and yon, ripping clumps of fat berries from branches that drooped with the load.

That's when the living seems easy up north, when the warmth and the bounty make summertime all that there is. Who thinks of winter when berries hang down? Every step on the trail brings a new clump that begs to be eaten. Who thinks of endless nights, snow drifts and ice when the beavers find cambium layers so soft and inviting?

If life can be easy up north, it is now, both for humans and the wild things they skulk through the forest observing.

Only bugs keep the good life in seasonal check. Deer flies, mosquitoes and midges seek blood, which can rein in euphoria fast.

So one goops on the lotion and walks into woods where the floor is a semi-damp sponge. A trail by the lake offers twice the enjoyment, where watchers can see summer creatures in two different zones.

The trail cuts through dark balsam fir habitat, interspersed with white birch and occasional giant white pines. Sun barely shines; sky is blue but not showing. Up top, where the cones on the balsams turn up, songbird peeps emerge sharp-edged but quickly fall muffled and still.

Who's up there? Don't think you can see anything. You must listen, and then you will know. Siskins and golden-crowned kinglets are there, and a red-breasted nuthatch in full nasal chorus — all birds of the summertime north. Out over the water, perched atop stunted spruce trees on a small rocky island, a loose flock of waxwings adds whispering songs to the mix.

There's no shortage here, not of bugs for bird gullets. The waxwings dip over the lake in a ceaseless ballet. Where the trail curls around a shallow, protected bay, white-tailed deer crash through shallows and bound toward the bugs and the woods.

Being a deer must be good when your belly's in water. It gets even better when succulent shoots just beneath the surface demand you dunk under to get them.

A common merganser and her nearly-grown brood swim as one where the marsh water deepens. She's done very well, bringing off eight survivors. The young stick like glue, but if all hell broke loose, they could probably fend for themselves.

She turns: they turn. This is synchonized swimming. She dives with a croak, reddish crest plastered down. They submerge. Life is following mom.

Bunchberries light up the trailside with bright orange flashes. Pine cone scales litter the top of a tree stump, where red squirrels ripped them from cones to devour their seeds.

Streams trickle down over dark, mossy boulders. Bugs whine; loons call on the lake.

What will the mood be here four months from now? Loons flown to the ocean? Beavers locked in their lodges? Methinks the wind might blow a bit.

And bears? They'll be sleeping quite fat in their dens, fortified by this year's berry crop.

MONTANA IS SO MANY THINGS

I have been to Montana and seen men make dirt mounds in cars. These were modern men, rugged men, men with the sense to know beauty. Bonding occurred with these guys, as we bummed through Big Sky Country, turning our rental van into a dumpster of sorts.

It's tough being neat, three amigos in search of adventure. If you're fishing, the gear can pile up pretty fast. Dirty boots filled with gravel, dank waders, trout nets — all get thrown in the back where they ripen by day and attract funky smells through the night.

Add a cooler, assorted clattering aluminum cans, camera bags, bird books and binoculars, and the landfill analogies can't be ignored for too long.

But we didn't care. Guys alone make a mess. You accept it and just move along. In Montana you move through magnificent land, land that dwarfs human efforts to tame it. Twist up through a mountain pass, hemmed in by steep canyon walls. A stream roars past boulders, hell-bent for the flatlands. Douglas firs cling to slopes mountain goats would need crampons to climb. Reaching the summit, you look down at one more hugh valley, flat as a pancake, stretching 10 miles or more between this mountain range and the next.

Any traffic around? Interstates here go begging for cars. Antelope browse their shoulders; horned larks hop out on them to snatch bugs that bake in the sun.

Drive and drive — cruise control — watching weather ahead: charcoal curtains of rain dumping torrents from one patch of sky. Cloudless sky over there, puffy clouds over there, thunderstorm over there — take your pick. The interstate chooses to head for the storm, 15 miles to the north and creating electrical chaos.

Shards of light, jagged bolts charged with neon descend. This is real lightning, not eastern stuff. The huge western sky shows it off to its fullest. Some bolts arch between clouds; others streak toward the ground, energized with destruction and fire. In a split second, dark skies explode into brightness. Strobe light fingers shoot down toward the earth, shining purple, not white.

What's that smell? Look up there, on the slope — those are flames in the rain. A bolt has flash-fried what was once a pine tree. A forest fire starts in a downpour that tries but can't quench it.

Any trout bum who views this bows down to the workings of nature. Life on the road isn't just catching fish; it is feeling a part of the grand western scheme of existence. Will my fish head amigos like birds? Yes, they will. They are men of the 90s, enlightened.

It's hard not to notice white pelican beauty, white as snow, skimming over the river. It is difficult driving past golden eagles standing in fields or long-billed curlews flying overhead or yellow-headed blackbirds atop cattail stalks in a marsh.

That's not to say brown trout aren't fun, sipping flies in the twilight. That's not to say rainbow trout don't gleam with unearthly beauty, their raspberry stripes slick as ice when they leap in the sun.

It's just that Montana is so many things — sage brush green, snow melt cool, sandhill cranes standing tall in a meadow. Amigos on holiday must open up wide, always blotting, retaining, recording the beauty that strikes them.

If there's dirt in the car, does it matter? It doesn't. Just keep the dead bugs off your window.

LADY BIRD'S PLACE

Bats, bugs and bluebonnets—man, I love Austin, Texas.

You can throw in Lady Bird Johnson, too. I love her. And throw in the Colorado River, deep green through the center of town.

Add them up, stir in Texas barbecue, chimney swifts buzzing yuppies on rooftop patio bars and fiddle music at the Broken Spoke saloon, and you have the first city in a long while that has made this cowpoke feel at home.

It helps to have Jungle Joe Brown as a friend. You can mooch off the man—take his bedroom, his car—and he still grabs the tab after dinner. You can ask that he jam on the brakes, then back up, then go forward, while roadrunners hunt bugs for their young.

Like the genie, Joe asks, "What would you like to see?" You respond that you want to see creatures and beauty: bats—half a million that hang from the Congress Avenue Bridge; armadillos—armed fortresses, rooting in shaded ravines; sprawling live oaks and a prickly pear cactus; deep holes you can swim in while waterfalls pound on your head.

You also say this: "I must see Johnson City, just 40 miles yonder, where LBJ roared over hill and dale driving his Lincoln." You also want Joe to check out Lady Bird—where she planted those gorgeous bluebonnets.

Austin roadsides are beautiful. For miles all around, they explode with bright colors—from bluebonnet blues in April to the warm reds of Indian blankets throughout all of May. Lady Bird did that. Thirty years ago, while some mocked her love of wildflowers, she worked to keep Texas beautiful. She lobbied for laws that banned billboards on scenic roads. She worked to plant wildflowers along rights of way. She kept the mad mowers from cutting and cutting again.

You tell Joe you want to drive some of her highways. You want to see blurs of bright yellow and red speeding by.

Like the genie, he tells you "no problem" and comes through in spades.

It is green there in east-central Texas hill country. It rolls ever gently, with limestone just under the soil. The air smells like juniper. Rivers teem with insect life. And here's the best part: Every bug that emerges has got something dying to eat it. During daylight, insect-eating swifts and swallows are a constant presence overhead. At night come the bats and the nighthawks.

I am telling you this: Austin has nighthawks.

If you're like Jungle Joe (who got his name on a Piper Club flight over 50 miles of unbroken Belizean jungle, during which he informed his fellow passenger that, should the engine conk out, there would be no place—repeat, no place—to land), then you normally go out at night to hear music or eat ice cream on a street corner. You don't look up often. You're not tuned to nighthawks.

But that strange eastern dude with the bird book, he knows. He can hear them on high, buzzing loudly. Hundreds and hundreds of nighthawks are up there. The glare from a car lot throws light on their ghostly white bellies.

Joe is enamored; he watches; his cone drips. He says we should go see the bats keep mosquitoes at bay.

We have previously mentioned Austin's half-million bats. The residents love them, pay homage, write stories, insist on their rigid protection. On any summer night, you can sashay along the park-like banks of the Colorado, toward the Congress Avenue Bridge, and see dozens, or hundreds, of people sitting on grassy banks, chatting. They are waiting for bats, Mexican freetail bats that arrive in Austin each spring, have their young and depart in the fall.

Around dusk the bats fly out from concrete grooves on the underside of the bridge's main deck, where they've slept, packed like sardines, all day. These grooves weren't built for bats; they just happen to be what a freetail bat thinks of as heaven.

At first there's one bat, then a second, then thousands—a fluttering cloud of bug busters determined to feed. The people below them are wearing short pants, because bugs in this town have a lifespan of one to two seconds. Go ahead; find me one old mosquito. Find me a human whose smooth exposed ankle has just felt a maddening stab.

You'll fail if you try. Bats have eaten the bugs. Joe Brown loves Austin's bats, and I guess that is why I love Austin.

HE LOOKED LIKE A GAUCHO

ECUADOR—He looked like a gaucho, replete with black hat, chaps and full grayish beard that flared out. That's what he was, sitting up on his pinto: a full-fledged South American cowboy, at home on Andean mountain slopes rendered slick by the season's hard rains.

But Stuart White was different. A man of means from the United States, he could have been anywhere and chose to be slogging through mud toward his ranch at the end of the earth.

No doubt there are places more isolated than the hacienda White and his wife, Lynn Hirschkind, maintain at 9,000 feet in the Ecuadoran Andes. It's just that most people don't see them.

Most people don't see because meeting these folks takes commitment. "Drive to the end of the road," they instruct you. Once you've gotten there — after six hours through axle-deep mud and tooth-jarring craters — you find your hosts waiting with a pack train of horses. Mount up and ride 3 1/2 hours up trails so muddy the horses sink down to their hocks. All the while you'll be climbing, clinging to slopes that seem too steep to farm but are not.

Swathed by mist, panchos pressed to their shoulders, peasant farmers hoe 45-degree slopes where potatoes have just started growing. Above them, perched on cliffs any condor would crave, mud-walled houses seep smoke from the kitchen fires burning within. Below, where the canyon cuts deepest, water roars toward a slow, flatter place on the lowlands. It tumbles, cascades, gouges, sweeps over boulders. The Rio Mazar doesn't rest.

One valley joins another. Two rushing streams merge as one. Slowly, the road and the car fade away in the fog.

Farmers work oxen across terraced contours. So steep are the slopes that one beast walks three feet below the other as the team pulls its plow through the soil.

"It was misty like this the first time we came here," Hirschkind says, turning back in her saddle. That was nine years ago. A newspaper advertisement had alerted the couple that a high mountain ranch was for sale. They climbed through the clouds and then bought it.

Since then, Hirschkind and White have become masters of self-sufficiency. Raising cattle, sheep, llamas and alpacas on 3,000 acres of pasture, cloud forest and tundra-like paramo, they have learned what it's like to have no one around but yourself.

When people get hurt near the ranch, they head straight for the modest hacienda where White and Hirschkind use sheepskin-covered stumps for chairs and build fires on a stone kitchen floor.

One woman came with a broken arm. They set it. On another occasion, the couple was called to a mountainside hut where a man lay with one leg in tatters. A boulder had fallen. Six men made a litter and carried him down the mountain, where a car bounced him over that terrible road to a town called Azoces and help.

The afternoon darkens as tales such as this fill the air. Mist transforms into pinpricks of rain. Two farmers clamber off their hillside plot to greet White effusively.

They have just finished a long day of plowing. He must join them for a trailside belt of cane liquor. White speaks with the men in fluent Spanish, joking, laughing, finally acquiescing as he pours down the potent clear liquid.

Darkness descends as we say our farewells. We are wet; we are cold — at 9,000 feet, three degrees south of the equator. The horses plod upward. They can't see their feet. Our host says they're very sure-footed.

Who is this man, perhaps in his late 40s, possessed of a doctorate in geography, who wanders these maintains as if his skin were coppery brown and he were born to them?

Who is this woman, wiry thin, black felt hat, raising Brown Swiss cattle instead of using her doctorate in anthropology to write papers and teach foreign ways?

A pinpoint of light cuts through mist up ahead. A cowbell clanks softly. "We're home," Stuart White tells his friends.

PART THREE
OTHER FRIENDS

SHE'S GOT WHAT IT TAKES

I will now report on my daughter's progress toward becoming a naturalist of extreme zeal and competence. Your job is to provide an unbiased assessment of her progress and tell me if I'm right in thinking she'll spend the rest of her life chasing frogs.

Maybe you've had a kid like this, or a brother, or sister. Maybe you, yourself, were one of these chosen people: an urchin type who loved dirt. If so, please advise as to whether the following play habits will persist through childhood, then evolve toward a life-long obsession with living things that aren't human.

For starters, the kid, at 5, loves every creature she's ever seen that waddles, slithers, flies or has fur. Penguins waddle. She wishes she could be one. Snakes slither. She'll eyeball a garter snake at 3 feet, then pronounce it a "curious creature." Birds fly. She imitates their wings with her arms. Of all God's creatures, ponies currently are riding highest.

Her field methods remain unrefined but show promise. To put it kindly, she collects overzealously. Huge clumps of wilted dandelions lie drying in various rooms. She does the same thing with daisies. Any flower that smells, she sticks in your face. You are constantly being presented with "bouquets." She listens attentively to talk of not picking, but with a 5-year-old's resolve, which tends to droop like wilting daisies.

Birds were her first love and remain a source of joy. Her eyes brighten when she sees them. When she dashes by a window — pigtails jouncing, on her way to do a puzzle or something — she always stops to look out. "There's a cardinal mommy with her babies." We get updates all the time.

As for identifying birds, the kid appears to be a list-maker. She likes knowing the full names of things. We never hear "hawk"; it's always red-tail or broad-wing. Hyphenated birds don't throw her. Two other favorites: the rose-breasted grosbeak and swallow-tailed kite.

Dirt and this child are one. If the dirt has been rained upon recently, all the sweeter for sculpting and probing. Lower forms of life, such as worms and millipedes, are removed from their mucky media and inspected carefully. All are deemed adorable. There are no ugly creatures on Earth, according to this naturalist.

Sartorially, the child seems suited to field work somewhere warm. Garments constrict her. She never wears shoes unless brow-beaten. If she could sport one bumper sticker, it would be, "No clothes beat any at all." When clothes are worn, their pockets attract rock fragments, grass blades and other natural wonders you and I might not find compelling. This kid finds everything compelling.

Perhaps she'll be a paleontologist. We've got the library for it. There must be 15 dinosaur books in the house. Fossil books, too. She calls the dinosaurs by their nicknames. "Bronta" is a current flame.

One recent morning, she woke me gently at 6:18 to report that a "mother deer" and two fawns were in the yard out back. I parted the curtains to peer through mist that hung like a rain forest cloak.

The doe munched grass and seemed pleased with the world. Her fawns swished their tails and looked new.

My little fawn loves the natural world, which pleases me more than I can say. Any of the world's great universities interested in refining that love and molding it, while offering financial aid, may contact me at leisure. We still have time. She's 5.

BARN MAESTRO

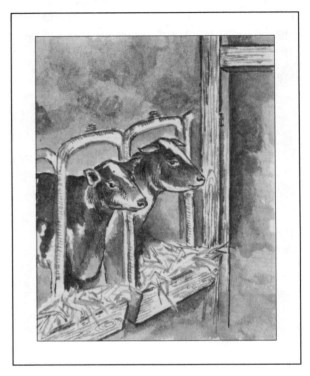

I was standing by a bitter cold lake recently when it hit me: I miss a good cow barn in winter. I miss all that warmth and not having to pay for the heat.

All alone by the lake, with the wind cutting through me, I felt sorely in need of the warmth Holsteins give when their sides nearly touch, swelling rhythmically next to each other. Chilled to the bone, I remembered the days when a barn beckoned to me, its dust-covered windows emitting a glow that could warm up a pre-dawn deep freeze.

Stan was the man in the barn all those mornings. Stan was an iron man, wiry and quiet, born with a calm resolution to never let hard work exhaust him.

His cows were all sweethearts, his reason for being, big tankers he doted upon. In the predawn he milked them while wind howled outside. Nailed to a post in the centermost aisle, a radio (cobweb-enshrouded) played loud country songs for the troops.

Oh, what a smell when you walked in that barn. Oh, what a feeling of moisture and life-giving warmth. It was good, by the way. It didn't smell good on your clothes two hours later, but it smelled like the heart of the earth when you first walked inside. Fifty-five cow bodies pumped out the heat. If you worked in that barn, you'd be down to a T-shirt in minutes.

Manure ker-plopped while Stan pushed a big cart past the noses of Bossy and Flo. Black muzzles glistened, necks clanked against stanchions, while Iron Stan scooped out a ration of pellets the Agway truck brought every month.

Then came the hay, horsed by hand to a hole in the floor over-head and dropped down to the bovines below. Take a bale, break it up, place it down where the noses can get it. Go get another, repeat, as you move down the line.

Suction machines clung to cow bags and pumped out a rhythm. While Stan clamped them on, I would climb up the silo and shovel down silage we'd made from field corn months before. Piled 30 feet high, the corn smelled sweet and sour — the vegetative equivalent of cider beginning to turn.

Dig in your pitch fork; throw down a big load. Do the same thing again until heaps of it lie on the cold concrete floor below.

Feed them hay, feed them pellets; make sure they get silage. Relieve them of milk so their bags can refill, and this same thing can happen again. Twice a day, every day, all these smells and sounds blended. Twice a day a cow symphony played while the maestro excelled.

Stan played conductor, a master of every part — mechanical, animal, vegetable. I played the grunt, sniffing deeply of cow smells, my muscles unable to cope.

The truth was I couldn't keep up with the maestro. In cow farming terms, I could barely pick up his baton. Morning milking would

end, and we'd walk through the cold toward his kitchen and mountains of food. After breakfast I'd sleep, tuckered out, while he cut
trees or thawed pipes or fixed roofs, never tiring.

This happened all year, unremitting, as seasons wheeled by. But
the winter was best, when those barn lights went on and the cow
breath hung heavy, and winter could not get inside.

HE CARVED WALKING STICKS

Pulled ever-slowly down deep tidal channels, we drifted along in his boat trolling lures for sea trout. North Carolina was icy that winter, possessed of a chill that could turn sunny days into frigid affairs on the coast. On the morning we fished, a north wind had purged clouds, and hard frost still encased the marsh grasses. Glare from the sun turned the morning sky silver, not blue.

Unfamiliar with sea trout and rumpled outdoorsmen, I pushed off with Leo to learn what young guys learn from old ones.

Leo wasn't that old, really; I wasn't that young. He just seemed older, because he was smarter, more experienced and more self-controlled. I knew next to nothing, except that I liked what he knew.

Sea trout, or weakfish, had been leaving the ocean to swim up tidal channels that winter. Leo announced we would troll through these channels in hopes fish and men would join forces to battle as one.

If memory serves, we caught nothing that day. But I did get to watch this older guy light his pipe and handle a boat and point out the white ibis flocks. Periodically, he would impart wisdom — about fishing, or having to work in an office all your life, or on cooking blue crabs so the meat steamed with juices. That usually occurred after the wind had kicked up, we had pulled in our lures and had angled toward shore to take five.

Tucked in the lee of a steep channel bank, we drank coffee from a stainless steel thermos that had taken on pewter's soft luster. Seated in the stern — his longish white hair and more longish mustache swirling slightly — Leo would tie up to the bank, cup a match in his hands, clasp his pipe in his teeth and proceed to touch flame to tobacco.

Without fail, he succeeded. Smoke raced from the dark wooden bowl through the bleached marshland grasses. Downwind, I could smell the rich blend and watch Leo draw slowly.

I liked how that old chamois shirt he wore looked. Its yellow had faded the color of sand dunes; its frayed cuffs and collar announced that he'd worn it for years. I liked the pipe, too — from the grain of the bowl to the stem he had gnawed like a dog chewing up an old bone.

Everything seemed natural about Leo — in the boat that cold morning; in my woods when he'd visit up north. When we fished he seemed part of the water, all sharp eyes and patience. When we walked in the forest, he never walked fast, always looking for mushrooms and such.

He carved walking sticks, which impressed me no end. They were beauties, rock-hard with a knot here or there, or a gnarl to infuse character. His cabin up north brimmed with natural things, such a snowshoes and ice fishing gear.

He showed me tents under pines, campfire flames in the dark and the smell of brook trout in a pan. When he moved south in winter, I followed him there, where he taught me to catch and clean sea bass and to bow down to big live oak trees.

Best of all, though, he sat in that boat, hunkered down with his pipe, loving every sweet breath that he took. From the bow I absorbed him, surrounded by salt grass, content to be here, nowhere else. This was his place, as the woods were up north. This was where things seemed to make the most sense, where a person could go to feel whole.

The man's outdoor spirit swept through me that day, just as sweet as the smoke from his pipe. Thank you, dear friend. I will pass on your torch to some puppy somewhere down the line.

CLEANING OUT HARRIET'S CAR

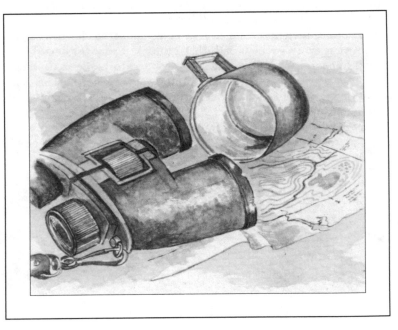

Harriet the birder cleaned out her car recently. As they do every five years or so, her friends crowded around to watch the ornithological equivalent of an archaeological dig.

Five years is about all a car can take under Harriet's care. She's a swamp loving, dirt road cruising, go-where-the-birds-are kind of lady, my mother is. Her cars pay the price. So whenever trade-in time rolls around, the birder's hot-line crackles with anticipation. Word spreads like wildfire that, once again, she'll be transferring a lifetime's accumulation of bric-a-brac from one vehicle to another.

Antiquarians exhibit a special interest in this great unearthing. Having witnessed past exhumations, they are well aware that items dating back to the dawn of binoculars often surface when Harriet probes the netherworld under her seats. Birding neophytes show great interest as well. They can watch the entire history of ornithology flash before their eyes as she digs through layers of paraphernalia that lie stratified in her trunk like sediments on an ancient sea floor.

What did she find this year? All manner of fascinating things. Some of it she even knew was there. For example, she knew there would be rumpled, unused checklists, two or three plastic cups that had lost their thermos companions, and a hand lens for ogling the working parts of wildflowers when birding moments turned slow. She also knew there would be maps: dozens of topographical maps, stuffed randomly into a clear plastic valise so as to defy all attempts to figure out which one was where.

Two hidden maps did surprise her. Digging through a layer that hadn't seen daylight for quite a while, Harriet came upon one that showed the boundaries of her territory during the 1958 Audubon Christmas Bird Count. Buried just below that, another map pinpointed the dark, soggy woods where a waterthrush sings every spring.

"Keep digging!" the assembled birders entreated. She was on a roll, they sensed. She had stuck an unmined vein.

Out came a pair of pruning shears no one had seen for decades. "I remember now," said Harriet. "I used them to borrow a little bittersweet from the cemetery." After the briefest of soul-searching moments, she also confessed to having blamed her husband—a saintly, patient man—for misplacing the shears when they turned up missing.

Unafraid, Harriet dug deeper. As the frost-heaved ground pushes stones toward the surface, so did more treasures bubble up. From nowhere came the paring knife she used for cutting watermelon on those hot summer field trips when the breeding bird atlas took all of her time. Then a camp ax appeared. A camp ax? All those assembled thought back fondly on Harriet's ax phase—a skull collecting phase—when her car would stop at all road-flattened creatures to assess their suitability for what was fast becoming an impressive collection of animal skulls. Next to appear was a very old Peterson field guide. The first 30 pages had eroded away. Then came a lens cap, dusty and splotched with grape jelly. "Isn't that Florence's lens cap?" a birding friend asked.

Harriet and her friend, Florence, had been birding the river on a winter's day several years ago. Way out in the middle, quite far from shore, a duck drifted by. It was not your average mallard, not a black duck or scaup. A ruddy duck, perhaps? The ladies' pulses quickened. Their eyes itched for optic assistance. The duck was drifting away, though, slipping downstream. Quickly, Florence, your telescope! In the hectic shuffle that followed, Florence's lens cap went the way of so many small things: down between a crack in the seats. Allowed to languish there, it wedged its way under a blanket. This wasn't just any blanket, it was Harriet's emergency blanket: the one she used when lying on her back fixing flat tires in the mud.

Harriet and Florence have had some very good times in mud. Seeing the blanket brought two of them back.

One time—it was late in the fall, all the warblers had gone—they got a flat in the boondocks and couldn't get the lug nuts off. Harriet jumped up and down on the tire iron, but it just wouldn't budge those lugs. A nice young man in a pickup came along and helped out. Another time, they got mired in ooze on a back country road that seemed to be going somewhere but wasn't. Bogged down to the axles, the pair trudged three miles to a farm. The farmer was busy but promised to come when he could. "I'll be there as fast as I can," he assured them. The ladies could trust him, he added. He was Presbyterian.

As they moseyed on back toward their car, Harriet and Florence saw thrushes you wouldn't believe: Swainson's thrushes, gray-cheeked thrushes, thrushes you don't often see bogged in mire.

Oh, the memories that emerged as my mother dug deeper. Each item brought back pages in a book of birding days. Remember when Harriet hooted like a barred owl into the pre-dawn blackness, and the damned thing nearly perched on her head? Remember all the heron rookeries, the migrating loons, the snowy owl in that windswept horned lark field?

Watching Harriet dig deeper, we remembered with smiles. Keep on trucking, Mom. We'll dig out again about five years from now.

RICK MARSI

WHEEL
OF SEASONS

An Award-winning Columnist
Reflects on the Natural Year

Illustrations by JAN MARSI

Foreword by David Rossie

RICK MARSI

Based at the *Press & Sun-Bulletin* in Binghamton, New York, Rick Marsi has been a syndicated columnist for Gannett News Service since 1981. A popular lecturer and outdoor instructor, Marsi released his first book of columns, *Wheel of Seasons*, in 1988.

JAN MARSI

An ordained minister in the United Methodist Church, Jan Marsi has been a freelance illustrator for 11 years. She divides her time between church activities and raising the Marsis' two children, Stephen and Kate.